Believing in Me

DEBORAH SOMORIN

Gill Books

Gill Books
Hume Avenue
Park West
Dublin 12
www.gillbooks.ie

Gill Books is an imprint of M.H. Gill and Co.

*Some names and identifying details have been
changed to protect the privacy of the people involved.*

9780717190638

Designed by Bartek Janczak
Edited by Neil Burkey
Printed by CPI Group (UK) Ltd, Croydon, CRO 4YY
This book is typeset in 12.25 on 19pt. Sabon

*The paper used in this book comes from the wood
pulp of sustainably managed forests.*

A CIP catalogue record for this book is available
from the British Library.

5 4 3 2 1

MIX
Paper from
responsible sources
FSC® C171272

To all of the people who believed in me

CONTENTS

Introduction   1

1   The calm before the storm   9
2   Roaming the streets   23
3   A good girl   39
4   Care   51
5   Rollercoaster   63
6   Home   81
7   Pregnant   97
8   Becoming a mother and losing mine   129
9   Seventeen   145
10   College   161
11   Adulting   177
12   Sharing my story   191

Resources   217
Acknowledgements   218

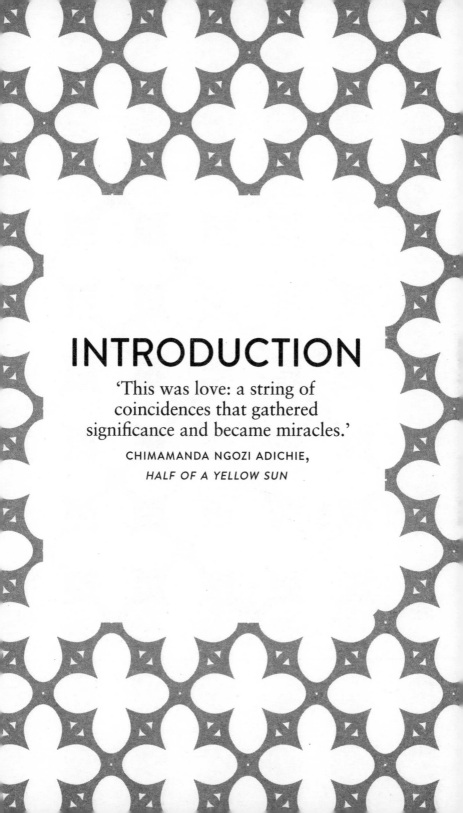

INTRODUCTION

'This was love: a string of
coincidences that gathered
significance and became miracles.'

CHIMAMANDA NGOZI ADICHIE,
HALF OF A YELLOW SUN

For all of us, our lives are journeys. Mine is no more remarkable than many others'. I like to say we all have 'our stuff' – periods in our life where we go through really tough times. I just happened to go through a lot of my 'stuff' at a young age. But I was very lucky. I knew that at the time, and I know that now.

I always seemed to have had one good adult who was watching over me. It was not always the same good adult, and they sometimes weren't even adults I knew personally. They were just individuals who were willing to do the right thing. I call them my disruptors. These are people who believed in me when I didn't believe in myself. They are people who believed in me when it seemed like no one else did. People who understood the unintended consequences of the systems they operated within, and actually cared enough about the impact these consequences had on people's lives to go through the effort of finding loopholes to alleviate those impacts. Why did they bother? I have no idea, but I'm so thankful to each one of them.

In 2017, the organisation I was working for asked me to feature in their graduate recruitment brochure. I felt really special to be chosen, not because I was Black, but because down the road from this fancy glass building was a night-time-only hostel I lived in when I was 13.

When the brochures came out, I couldn't believe my picture was picked to feature on a page of its own. I remembered how I admired the women in these brochures when I was in college, and I couldn't believe I was now one of them. I emailed all the organisations that supported me when I was living in homeless hostels or care homes. I told them that my son Liam and I would be eternally grateful to them for the support they provided to us over the years, and included a link to the brochure.

Seeing the brochure was the first time I stopped and actually realised what I had accomplished through perseverance during some very tough years. It might seem strange that this didn't sink in at my graduation, or even when I got my job. The best way I can describe it is that I felt like I was on autopilot. I just kept trying to survive each day, no matter what hardships came with it. I was determined to make something of myself so that I could support my son. He needed me, and I didn't want him to ever need anything I couldn't provide.

After I sent the email, one of the organisations asked me to share my story with donors so they could understand the impact their donations could have on people's lives. Somewhat reluctant at first, I gradually came to the realisation that parts of my story are important and need to be heard. My fervent hope is that my story will both connect with people who have been where I've been and raise the awareness amongst those who have not. This book will take you on my journey from living in a homeless hostel at 13 and getting pregnant at 14 to becoming a chartered accountant and making it onto the *Forbes* 30 under 30 list a decade later.

None of us know how much we can handle until our personal resilience is put to the test. When I went through the worst times in my life, there was no grand plan I was following. I constantly doubted myself. In college especially, I had this narrative stuck in my head of 'Who do I actually think I am to think I can get a degree? If teen moms and care leavers became chartered accountants en masse, I would know. So, who am I to think I'm special enough to be the exception to the statistics?' Even with a degree and a master's in accounting behind me, this narrative still plagued me when I did my Final Admitting Examination to Chartered Accountants Ireland.

But I wanted to stand on my own two feet. I wanted to be able to provide anything my son needed. I didn't want those who didn't believe I could do this to be right. I had to aim beyond what I even felt I was capable of. I had no other choice, or at least at the time it felt that way. I felt like I had to keep going to survive.

Chapter 1

THE CALM BEFORE THE STORM

'May you never forget what is worth remembering, or remember what is best forgotten.'

IRISH PROVERB

My story begins with my mother's story. I want you to meet her and discover the person she was, but I must admit that part of me is apprehensive of you judging her and her life, which could never be packaged up neatly and presented to you.

My mum grew up in Nigeria in the 1980s. Her mother was more progressive than most. She had travelled to the UK in her youth to train and work as a nurse. When she returned to Nigeria, she worked, married twice and had four children: Tunde, Ladi, Oriyomi (my mum) and Bukki. She planned for the future, working her way up to a senior nursing position and securing a pension. She even bought an investment property to provide her with additional rental income when she retired. My mum was lucky to grow up with a strong independent woman as a role model.

My mum was the perfect child: studious, always doing what she was told and never getting in trouble. When I did something wrong, like talk back to her, she would say, 'I didn't kill my mother, so don't kill me.' I think she meant that she didn't stress out her mum, so I shouldn't stress her out either. When my mum finished college, she decided to start a small business. She set up a shopfront at the front of her mum's house, where she sold soft drinks and snacks. She also offered catering services to private parties and worked with a tailor to make custom outfits for special occasions.

The catering service is how she met my dad. He attended a private party that she was catering. He said it was love at first sight for him, and described her as the most beautiful woman he had ever met, even to this day. My dad pretty much swept my mum off her feet. He brought her to fancy meals and fancy events and bought presents to impress her. He even gave money to her family to help take care of them. He was keen to marry her as soon as possible to officially take her off the market, and so my mum and dad got married after about a year of dating.

Years later, after they were married, if they were fighting, my mum would often tell me about how she could have married two other really wealthy men but instead chose to marry my father. I would roll my eyes and wonder why she was telling me this. In hindsight, I realise my father was probably within earshot when she made these remarks. My dad had trained and worked as a chartered accountant in the UK. I imagine that my mum thought this might have made him less beholden to the patriarchal Nigerian standards of how women and wives should behave. To a certain extent it did, but keeping with Nigerian societal customs and expectations also mattered to him.

We lived in the UK on and off while I was growing up. I was born in London in 1993, my brother Michael was born in Nigeria a year later and my sister Mary was also born in London a few years after that. My dad had been married twice before he met my mother, and his kids from his second marriage weren't all adults yet when my parents got married, so I think he wanted to be close by for that reason. Really close. Our family home was in Festac, a town in Lagos. It was down the road from the old home my dad shared with his second family. He had two kids with his first wife and five children with his second wife. His first wife's kids had been really lovely to his second wife's kids. But his third wife's kids – me and my siblings – were apparently not so lucky. When I was growing up, his second wife's kids were always around. I sensed tension between them and my mum, but I never really understood why. I was just so excited that my cool older siblings were visiting.

At the time, my dad was a chartered accountant and a Shepherd of the Celestial Church of Christ in Festac. A shepherd is like a pastor. As you can imagine, I had a pretty conservative upbringing as a result. Sundays were for church, and not just for an hour – we had church all day. Bedtime stories were bible stories. TV shows like *Sabrina the Teenage Witch* were banned. Wearing black or red was also a big no-no – these were the devil's colours, and I would be inviting trouble into my life by wearing them.

My mum ran a little shop in the church, where she sold soft drinks and snacks. She always looked so beautiful and had so much grace and presence. I remember all eyes being on her any time she entered a room. Red Door by Elizabeth Arden was her signature scent, and she loved to wear gold jewellery. Even when she didn't have make-up on, she looked amazing. My dad adored her and us.

We were a normal middle-class family, and I had a relatively happy upbringing until I was about eight. My mum and dad were approaching their tenth anniversary, when they started having huge blow-up fights, more and more frequently. My dad had always let my mum get her own way, but something now just felt different, like they were fighting about something he was refusing to back down on. I later found out they were fighting about how his second wife's kids treated me and my siblings. They felt that their dad's home was their home, and that they could treat it as such, regardless of whether they were being disrespectful to me, my siblings or my mum. I think my dad felt bad about the fact that he had remarried and had three more children and was living in bliss down the road from his other kids. My mum and granny told me that this created a lot of tension between my parents, and eventually my dad started refusing to eat dinner at home. He instead ate with my mum's married best friend (or that's at least what my mum told me).

My mum got really down, and started to stay in bed all day. She locked her door so we couldn't see or talk to her. Now I can see she was clearly suffering with depression. We had a phone book beside the telephone in our house. We wrote phone numbers of family and friends in there. One day, I got fed up just walking past a locked door every day when I came home from school, so I opened the phone book and tried to call anyone I could think of who would be able to help me convince my mum to come out of her room. They came, sat outside her door and tried to convince her to come out. I didn't call anyone from my dad's side of the family because we were never really that close to them. When my dad came home from work and saw all these people sitting outside my mum's room, he just walked past silently. I could tell he was embarrassed to find them there. Ultimately, he got a carpenter to take my mum's door off its hinges. He told everyone it was a family matter – and they left. My mum's room smelled like she had been throwing up, and I thought that maybe she was just sick and that was why she had locked herself in her room. I remember feeling really sad and confused. My friends tell me I even spoke to them at school about what was going on, but I don't remember those conversations. What I do remember is that there was a period of temporary calm after that. The calm before the storm.

And the storm did come. I still remember how surreal it was standing on the balcony watching my mum smash all the windows of my dad's car. She then came into the house and started smashing all the TV screens. My dad was at work, and I wasn't sure where my mum had been, but clearly something had happened to make her snap. She quickly packed what she could. I remember us leaving, but I had no idea where we were going. My siblings and I were herded into a taxi and arrived at my granny's place a few hours later. My mum had no car, no money and barely any clothes for us. My granny was a pensioner with a subsidised income but not enough to support my mum and her three children under 10.

My granny tried to play peacemaker with my mum and dad, but his family didn't want them back together. They refused to let my mum and granny into the house to just try to talk it out with him. At some point in all the chaos, my siblings and I moved back in with my dad, while my mum stayed with my granny. We weren't allowed to see or speak to my mum during that time, which I can only imagine was very tough for her. It was incredibly tough for me. I didn't think it was fair that my mum couldn't see her kids, and although we butted heads, she was the only mum I had. Of course I loved and missed her, as did my siblings.

I was getting ready to leave for school one day when I collapsed with stomach pains and was rushed to the hospital. Being rushed to hospital was something I was kind of used to as a child. My brother Michael and I suffered with really bad asthma as kids. We often woke in the middle of the night unable to breathe, and we had to use a machine called a nebuliser to be able to breathe properly again. My parents had one, but if we were both up having an asthma attack, one parent would need to stay home to use our machine and the other would need to bring me to the hospital to use another machine there. This time, I wasn't going to the hospital because of my asthma, and neither of my parents could be with me. I remember being terrified, and just wanting my mum to be there.

On the same day, my mum had arrived at the school and refused to leave without her kids. The school contacted my dad, who was hundreds of kilometres away in Abuja for work. He asked that the school be locked down until she agreed to leave without my siblings, which the school agreed to do. This meant that nobody could come in or out to pick up their kids after school. This was only sustainable for so long, however, and she was eventually allowed to leave with them. My dad probably assumed he would be able to get them back when he returned. But he was wrong. With minimal money and resources, my mum had bought plane tickets. She had intended to take me with her, but as chance would have it, I was in a hospital bed doubled down in pain, hours away from any airport.

For my mum, leaving was the only choice she had left if she wanted to keep her kids. Even if it meant leaving me behind with my dad, she had to protect the two she had with her – and the one she had on the way.

A letter to Debbie in the hospital

Debbie,

This is a letter from your 28-year-old self. I know being in this hospital room without your parents is really scary. You're trying to be brave, but even as an adult, you want your mum to hold your hand and tell you everything will be okay when you go to the hospital. So don't feel like you're weak for being scared and missing your mum. I know you miss your siblings too. You think you'll see them soon, but your mum and dad are going through something right now. It's hard to explain why, but you're not going to speak to or see your mum, brother or sister for a while. I know you're hoping you will all just go back to being one big happy family soon, but that's not possible. Life will never go back to normal, but I want you to hang in there and know you're going to be okay.

Lots of love,
Your future self x

Chapter 2

ROAMING THE STREETS

'Joy is sometimes a blessing, but it is often a conquest.'

PAULO COELHO, *BY THE RIVER PIEDRA
I SAT DOWN AND WEPT*

I stayed with my dad for a year, during which time I wasn't allowed to speak to my mum, which meant I couldn't speak to my siblings. My dad didn't really talk to me about what was going on, and I missed them a lot. I'm the oldest sibling, which meant that when my parents weren't there, I had been in charge. It had been my responsibility to make sure my siblings gathered at the meeting spot when school was finished so that we could go home together. My brother was always late finishing his schoolwork, so I usually went back into the school building to get him. I missed being able to do little things like that.

I don't really remember too much from this time, but I think that people in school noticed that I was sad, and that's why my principal allowed me to take a call from my mum in her office one day. I had never been in the principal's office up to this point because I was always well-behaved at school. When I got there, she told me that my mum was on the phone. I finally got to speak to her! We didn't get to chat for long, and I cried the whole time. My mum told me that she was okay, that she was in Ireland, and that I had a baby brother, whose name was Solomon. My mum's words replayed in my head for weeks after that, and not being able to tell my dad what I knew was really difficult. But at some point, my mum and dad started talking to each other again, and Dad told me about Solomon himself, so I didn't have to pretend I didn't know anything anymore. I think he could see how sad I was being away from my siblings, so he agreed with my mum that I would join her in Ireland.

When my dad told me about the trip, he said we were just going on a holiday so that I could see my siblings. I vividly remember getting out of the taxi in Naas, where my mum was living. Michael and I ran to give each other the biggest hug. I was delighted to be reunited with my siblings, and we had so much catching-up to do. I wanted to hear all about their new life here – if they had made friends, what school was like, that type of thing. Most importantly though, I was excited to meet my new baby brother Solomon for the first time.

At some point during the trip, I remember my dad pulling me aside for a chat. He told me that I wouldn't be coming home with him, and I would be staying in Ireland with my mum. My mum and I had got along so far on my trip, but I didn't know how things would go once he wasn't around. He assured me that he would stay in contact and come back to visit as often as he could. But I can't say that I didn't feel abandoned by my dad at this time. He had just turned 60, and I think he just couldn't cope with raising a teenage girl by himself.

My mum enrolled me in Fifth Class in the girls' Catholic school in Naas town. I still remember everyone staring at me when I arrived on my first day. I imagine it's similar to how animals at the zoo feel. When you're 10, you don't have the right skills to rationalise those types of experiences.

From day one, I felt like a freak. Kids would openly comment on how big my lips were or how dark my skin was, and I didn't know how to process those interactions. These comments eventually became my own self-deprecating narrative. I don't hold a grudge against any of those kids, because that's exactly what we all were – kids. On reflection, my one regret is not talking to my mum about what was going on, because she would have given me advice on how to deal with mean comments. My mum and I just didn't have the type of relationship where we chatted about things like that.

As a good African daughter, I was expected to get up, get dressed, help get my siblings dressed, help make breakfast for everyone, go to school and return immediately home. When I got home I was to dedicate the rest of my day to homework, looking after my siblings and doing domestic chores like helping my mum make dinner. I was not to be 'roaming the streets', as my mum put it, or playing with my friends. My mum constantly reminded me of these expectations and any time I fell short, she would scream at me or hit me. Hitting disobedient children isn't unheard of in Nigerian families. (It's similar to Irish families who had a wooden spoon for spanking naughty children back in the day.) But my mum always took it too far with me. It was like she took her built-up frustration out on me, and I don't know why.

It wasn't until I went into Sixth Class that I started rebelling. I made new friends who smoked, drank and did other fun things that we were not supposed to be doing at our age. My mum was not a fan of any of my friends, and even though she didn't really know the extent of what we got up to, she still had a bad impression of them. I obviously did not share her apprehensions, and this led to huge fights between us. It also led to her banning me from hanging out with these friends. Of course, that just made me want to hang out with them more – I just had to become a bit sneakier about how I would get to spend time with them.

Some of us signed up to become altar servers, which meant we could go to town at the weekend or after school and sneak behind the back of the church and smoke for the duration of the altar-serving lesson without our parents knowing. Because I attended a Catholic school my mum was okay with me attending altar-serving lessons. It became a routine on a Friday that after school we would go into the toilets of the McDonald's beside our school and get changed into our ra-ra skirts, throw in our clip-in hair extensions, do our make-up and spritz perfume all over ourselves. Then we'd march into town thinking we were the best thing ever.

I got away with this for a very long time before I got caught. There was one particularly funny close call though. Mum went to a redeemed church – a Pentecostal church – so she had no reason to come to Catholic Mass to make sure that I was there. But on one occasion she decided to do just that. Thankfully, the priest was really nice, and he let me serve during the Sunday Mass service she attended. I obviously didn't tell him that my mother thought I had been doing this for months. We were at the end of the Mass and I was just starting to relax, thinking I had got away with it, when the priest said something along the lines of 'And well done to Deborah on her first altar-serving. She's done a great job.' He probably thought that it was nice to say that for my mum's benefit, but I just wanted the ground to swallow me up – I was caught! And dead! To my surprise, my mum hadn't heard the bit about it being my first time (or maybe she pretended not to) and was just so proud that the priest had said my name.

The day I did get caught my mom was in town at the post office. I was with my friends and some boys when we locked eyes as she came out of the post office. I could see the shock on her face – I don't think she realised I owned hair extensions, make-up or a top as low-cut as the one I was wearing. She came over to me and ordered me home.

I knew what was coming. I knew I was going to get a beating. The Bible states:

> *Withhold not correction from the child: for if thou beatest him with the rod, he shall not die. Thou shalt beat him with the rod, and shalt deliver his soul from hell [i.e. death]* – Proverbs 23:13–14

As I said, spankings and beatings weren't uncommon in African households, even in the ones outside Africa. My home wasn't any different. After everything my mum had been through, she felt disappointed and frustrated with me. I was selfish, as 11-year-olds tend to be, and I didn't see things from her perspective. However, the problem here wasn't a child being punished for being out of control. It was a mother going beyond that and taking her frustration out on a child. By the time I went into care shortly after this, I had scars all over my body.

I obviously didn't tell people what was going on at home. But the angrier her beatings became, the more I craved the feeling of escape I had when I hung out with my friends. The night I went into care, I had snuck off to hang out and drink some alcopops with my friends in a nearby estate. The older kids in our group stayed out till around 11 or 12 p.m. My curfew was eight o'clock – if my mum even knew that I had gone out, that is. Once I was out past curfew, I knew I was in trouble anyway, so I just stayed out so I could enjoy being with my friends before I had to go home to face the music.

When I came home that night, I was past curfew and there was no key in the usual spot or sign of my siblings to help sneak me in. I had no choice but to ring the doorbell. I knew I was in a huge amount of trouble but my only other option was to sleep outside in the cold. Mum opened the upstairs hallway window and asked where I had been, and with whom. I wouldn't tell her, because I knew that would land me in worse trouble. She told me to go back to my friends, because she wasn't letting me in for the night. I pleaded with her to let me in until she poured a bucket of water on me. I left and went to my friend Róisín's house. I explained to her and her parents what had happened. Her parents got me a towel to dry off with and said I could sleep on the couch. As I lay there in the darkness, the reality of the situation set in. I felt so embarrassed. *Why hadn't I just gone home on time?*

As my mind raced through what would happen next, the doorbell rang. It was the Gardaí – my mum had called them. My mum really hated Róisín but guessed she would be the first friend I would go to for help after I left. I don't know why she would have refused to let me in only to then call the Gardaí when I eventually left, but I assume maybe she was hoping it would scare me, and they would just bring me back home. But I actually ended up going into care that night. I don't think any major alarm bells were ringing at this stage; I think they just wanted us to have a bit of space so my mum could cool down. I later found out that I was taken into care under Section 12 of the Child Care Act, which didn't require a court order to temporarily 'remove [a] child to safety'.

From the moment the Gardaí arrived at Róisín's house, I felt like I was having an out-of-body experience, watching things happen that couldn't possibly be happening to me. I had to be watching them happen to someone else. The car ride to the Garda station I had never been inside of. Waiting with the Gardaí for the duty social worker to arrive. Being taken in the middle of the night to the emergency foster home in Dublin. Getting into pyjamas that weren't mine. Lying down on a bed that wasn't mine. I didn't understand how I had caused all this just because I wanted to stay out with my friends.

A few days later, I got a medical, as is normal for kids coming into care. That's when the doctor noted injuries and scars consistent with physical abuse. And that's when the alarm bells started ringing.

A letter to Debbie after the medical

Debbie,

This is a letter from your older self. I've thought about what my life would have been like if Dad had taken me back to Nigeria with him. I wonder if I would have had a more normal and stable childhood. But I believe that everything happens for a reason. In the future, you will have an incredible child called Liam who brings so much joy and happiness into your life. That wouldn't have been possible if you'd left with your dad.

You're in a mental space right now where hanging out with your friends means so much to you because it's a break from the reality of what has been going on at home. You know that the longer you stay out with your friends, the worse the punishment is when you go home. This time other adults got involved, and they've said that you can't go home right now. I know you feel really guilty, like you've done something wrong and brought unnecessary attention to your mother's door. But you've done nothing wrong. You're 11. There are other ways to communicate with a child who is pushing boundaries and acting out without beating them. I know this is how your mum was raised, but things are different now. You deserve to be safe – everyone does. So please stop blaming yourself for bringing additional stress into your family's life.

Lots of love,
Your future self x

Chapter 3

A GOOD GIRL

'If we believe that tomorrow will be
better, we can bear a hardship today.'

THICH NHAT HANH

My social worker went to court to request an emergency court order to take me into care for 14 days. While I can understand the emergency nature of the intervention, it makes me sad that the social workers didn't communicate better with my mum when I first went into care. Like me, she had no idea how this whole situation was going to play out and, more importantly, no guidelines on what she had to do to help fix things. I've never spoken to my father about what my mother told him at this time, but I assume that it was very little.

As nobody knew how long I would be in care, a series of short-term foster placements were sought for me while the social workers figured out if the situation with my mum was fixable. What followed was a merry-go-round of foster placements, so many in such a short time that they all blended into one another. Over the next nine months, I stayed with six separate foster families for varying periods of time. If the social work team had hoped to renew my sense of security and belonging, then this approach certainly didn't work. In no particular order, I went from Naas to Clondalkin, from Maynooth to Lucan, and from Tallaght to Celbridge, with the longest stay in these homes being about three months and the shortest less than two weeks. At no time did I know how long I would stay or where I would be going next. My social worker would simply show up and inform me that I would be leaving.

I didn't blame my social worker for the situation. I would go on to have several different social workers over the coming years, but my foster placement social worker was lovely and is the only one I still stay in touch with.

I only have vague memories of this time. The first foster family was nice. They brought me to get pyjamas, clothes to last me a few days and some toiletries. The next foster family had a Labrador, and I was terrified of even little dogs at the time. At the start, I thought I would never come out of my room, but by the time I was leaving that dog and I were the best of friends. The next family had me cook for their children, who were around eight and nine, and left me in the car anytime they needed to go into town. I was really well-behaved in these homes, partly because they were never in Naas, so I was very far away from my drinking buddies, but mainly because I was carrying so much guilt about the amount of hassle I had caused. I wanted to go home and I wasn't allowed to – it felt like that was all my fault! I didn't really understand what was going on, but I wanted to go home.

I felt like the worst person on the planet for causing all this and bringing so much stress to my mum's door. I missed my siblings, and I didn't like feeling like a stranger in someone else's home. But that's what foster care felt like to me. No matter how much effort was put in, there was always a difference in how affectionate a family was with their own children. It just made me miss my family even more.

I wasn't allowed to see my mum and siblings initially, but eventually we got to have more frequent visits. These were called 'access' visits. My mum was being really nice, and we were finally getting on. I still have a letter I wrote to a judge ahead of one of the court dates to get another care order for me. On the front of it I had written:

> *Dear Mummy,*
> *Will you please hand this to the judge? I*
> *love you and I have been a good girl.*
> *From your loving daughter Deborah*
> *Somorin*

I guess my mum had to jump through certain hoops to get me back. When she did, I was allowed back home after a few months. Things were okay for a bit, but my mum had grown to resent me for talking to my social worker about the beatings. She constantly painted me as the source of anything that was going wrong in her life, and my siblings started to do the same. While there wasn't any more physical abuse, the emotional abuse was worse. I felt like she hated me. Within a few months, our relationship had broken down again, and I was taken back into care by my social worker.

This time, I didn't go to a foster family. I went to a residential care home just outside Dublin. Generally speaking, foster placement tends to be for younger children – pre-teens for the most part – and as I was fast approaching the end of that age bracket, the list of available options was getting shorter. The decision to place someone in a residential home is seismic. Once you are in that system, it becomes very hard to extricate yourself from it and work your way back to some sort of normal life. I'm not saying that it's impossible, and I would like to think of myself as proof of that, but it makes the journey back so much more arduous. The residential care system in this country is a very blunt tool. It is not really designed to cater for and address individual or complex interpersonal problems. It's also a mixed bag. You have kids who broke their curfews living with teenagers who have already done a stint in prison (well, juvenile prison).

What should have been happening at that stage is that the social workers should have been doing everything they could to stop me from entering that system. They should have worked with my mother and me to fix our problems. They weren't insignificant, but they certainly weren't irreparable. I feel that there was an unwillingness to engage or understand. The fact that we had come from a different country and a different culture created a barrier, not from our side, but from theirs.

My mother was very outspoken about wanting me back. I think she would have tried to challenge the system and break down the barrier. I wonder if the system found it challenging to relate to my mother. I wouldn't be surprised if that was the case, but I'm not sure that any of this was a direct result of her culture, and even less so her colour. I do believe, however, that these were factors in terms of how we were related to and dealt with by social services. At a time when my family needed more help and intervention – counselling and family therapy would have been more appropriate responses – the path of least resistance was chosen instead, and as a result, our family would never fully recover.

In an ideal scenario, I would have gone into a foster placement, and then social services would have worked with my mother to prepare the way for my return. Instead, due to the lack of a suitable foster placement and even less intervention with my mother, the decision was made to place me in residential care. The gravity of this situation – of how I was disappearing further down the rabbit hole of the care system – didn't occur to me at the time, not least because I was glad to be back in Naas after my whirlwind tour of other people's houses. I had just started First Year in secondary school, and I was planning to get my shit together. I just put my head down and tried not to be a hassle to anyone so that I could go back home eventually. Naas felt like home, or at least as close to home as I'd known for a while. I knew people there, and although I wasn't in my family home, they weren't too far away. Also, it was where my friends were. Unfortunately, this is pretty much where the advantages of the situation ended.

A letter to Debbie entering residential care

Debbie,

You're feeling hopeful that this new move will provide some stability. You're also happy to be close to your mum and siblings again. It seems like you'll have more freedom to hang out with your friends too in this new home. Unfortunately, the year ahead is one that you will later wish never happened. At times, it will feel very lonely and you won't feel safe. Listening to Kelly Clarkson's *Breakaway* CD on your Discman will be your safe haven. It's because getting knocked down and finding the strength to get back up again is the theme of a lot of songs on that album. You'll feel completely broken at times, but I promise things will get better.

Lots of love,
Your future self x

Chapter 4

CARE

'If you can't fly, then run. If you can't run, then walk. If you can't walk, then crawl. But whatever you do, you have to keep moving forward.'

MARTIN LUTHER KING JR

Residential care homes for children are dotted all over the country. The most recent survey by Tusla, published in November 2018, states that there are 157 residential homes for children in the Republic of Ireland. There are some large centres, like Oberstown or Ballydowd, but most of them are run in normal residential houses. Some of these are run by voluntary organisations, and others are privately owned. Regardless of management, they are all regulated and subject to inspection by Tusla. Any child in the care system can be referred to one of these homes, and if the funding is approved, then that is where the child will live. The length of their stay is governed by the allotment of funding and by the length of the care order. Care orders are only ever granted by judges in court. An emergency care order allows for a maximum of eight days in care, an interim care order allows for a maximum of 28 days in care (but can be extended) and a supervision order allows for a maximum of 12 months (but can also be extended).

Children's residential centres are often regular domestic homes in housing estates in villages, towns and cities, and occasionally in rural areas. These centres typically house between two and six children and usually accommodate teenagers, as opposed to younger children. The homes are staffed by social care workers, and this is important to remember, because 'social care worker' can often be confused with 'social worker'. While these two professions often work side by side, they are completely different in character and function. A social worker is someone who works for social services, providing help and support for people who need it. Social workers are responsible for intervening in domestic crises and have the power (in tandem with the Gardaí) to place young people into care. The social care worker is the person who works with the young person in a residential care home. Social care workers look after all aspects of the day-to-day care of young people, ranging from cooking and cleaning to statutory recording and reporting.

My new home was one in a chain of for-profit residential care homes. I lived in this home just outside Dublin when I started First Year. That was one of the worst years of my life, and I still wear the scars to this day. That home was where I met my next abusers.

There were only two other residents living in the care home when I moved in. I'll call them Karen and Maria. They had been there for years and had strong relationships with the care workers who looked after us. They both had violent histories and, unfortunately, they weren't thrilled with my arrival. They called me the N-word, locked me out of the house when I came home from school and looked for every opportunity to try to attack me. The care workers tried to keep me safe. They even slept outside my door at night to prevent the girls from coming into my room to hurt me while I slept. Although there was another care home down the road with beds available, owned by the same company, I wasn't moved, so this hell went on for months. But then I met someone I'm going to call Luke.

Luke lived in another care home owned by the same company. He was nearly 18 and getting ready to move out into his own apartment. I'd overheard the girls talking about him, so I knew they both had a crush on him before I met him. One day, I came home from school to see that the girls had barricaded the front and side doors to prevent me from being able to enter the care home. This wasn't the first time this had happened. I could hear the care workers inside convincing them to let me in. Then Luke arrived. Karen and Maria let him in straight away, of course, but Luke realised what was going on and asked that they also let me in. He convinced them to do just that and he also – somehow – convinced them to start being nice to me.

Scared that they could turn on me again at any time, I followed them around and did whatever they asked. Myself, Maria and Karen would all hang out together watching TV or just chatting in the kitchen when Luke came over. Soon, Luke had my number and we were texting. Honestly, I initially thought he was just someone looking out for me like a big brother. But then I started getting messages about how much he liked me. I didn't want the girls to start being mean to me again if I told him I saw him as a big brother, not a crush. I didn't really know what to do, but I eventually decided not to make things any more difficult for myself. I didn't seek out his attention, but I didn't rebuff any I received either.

When he turned 18, he got an apartment near the housing estate I was living in. I was still a virgin, but he was keen to change that after he moved into his new place. I wasn't ready. I had read that there would be blood, and was scared it would hurt. I didn't want my first time to be with him, but I didn't want the girls to start being mean to me again either.

He arranged everything, including where and when we would meet to avoid getting caught. The day finally came, and I felt sick as I walked over to his apartment after school. As he had asked, I was careful not to be seen walking into his building.

He opened the door and we went straight to his bedroom. I felt gross. I just wanted it to be over so I could go home. It hurt, just like I thought it would. I kept thinking, *should I tell him it hurts? Maybe if I tell him he can do it another way that won't hurt?* After he was done, he reached for his phone. His face dropped and he was suddenly very panicked. One of the care workers from his home had texted to say she was on her way over to him. He asked me to hurry up and get dressed and leave, so that she wouldn't find me there or see me walking out of his building. I guess this is when I realised that Luke didn't like me, he just wanted to use me for sex.

After that, he still came over to our house all the time, but he didn't talk to me anymore and he stopped texting me. Eventually, the girls started being mean to me again. At some point, something changed and he started getting worried I would tell someone. To be honest, I was just happy he had left me alone and I wouldn't have to have painful sex with him again. I remember watching TV in the sitting room on my own one day. Luke came in, shut the door behind him and punched the couch right beside my face. He said that was what he would do to me if I told anyone what had happened.

I was terrified, and I knew I had to get out of that house. At my next social worker check-in, I couldn't find the words. We got through the whole visit without me saying anything. She drove me home, and I still remember us sitting at a traffic light five minutes from my care home when I blurted it out. At that moment I was suddenly really scared that nobody would believe me and that he would find out I had said something and come hurt me. But, unbeknownst to me, the fact that Luke had a thing for 12-year-olds was apparently not news to my care workers. Luke had been living with a 12-year-old girl in his care home before he turned 18. He had been sneaking into her room and having sex with her too. But that had just come to light. This explained his sudden paranoia; I assume he didn't want me to corroborate her story.

I was moved to another home after that, primarily because Luke had a history of violence (also news to me), and the care workers felt that they couldn't keep me safe if he tried to break in while we slept. Afterwards, the guards visited me a couple of times to take my statement, but I wouldn't talk to them. At the time, I blamed myself in part for what happened. I hadn't said no, and I had gone to his apartment willingly. I had provided my consent. I didn't understand that 12-year-olds can't consent to having sex with 18-year-olds. That's statutory rape, and he was old enough to know that what he was doing wasn't right. I had just wanted the bullying from the other girls to stop. Nobody else had been able to convince them to leave me alone. I felt like I owed him for that.

A letter to Debbie after moving
to the care home

Debbie,

This wasn't how you imagined your first time having sex. You wanted to meet someone nice and lose your virginity to someone you loved. You were also definitely not ready. You are still a child, even though you feel a lot more grown up. You only spoke up because you were scared he would hurt you, but you don't think he should go to prison because you gave consent.

It's only after years of counselling that I now understand that he groomed you and took advantage of you while you were vulnerable. You were simply too young to consent, and he knew that. The situation with the girls bullying you in that house went on for far too long, and you should have been moved long before Luke came into the picture. I don't know why that situation was allowed to go on for as long as it did, but thankfully you are in a safer environment now.

Lots of love,
Your future self x

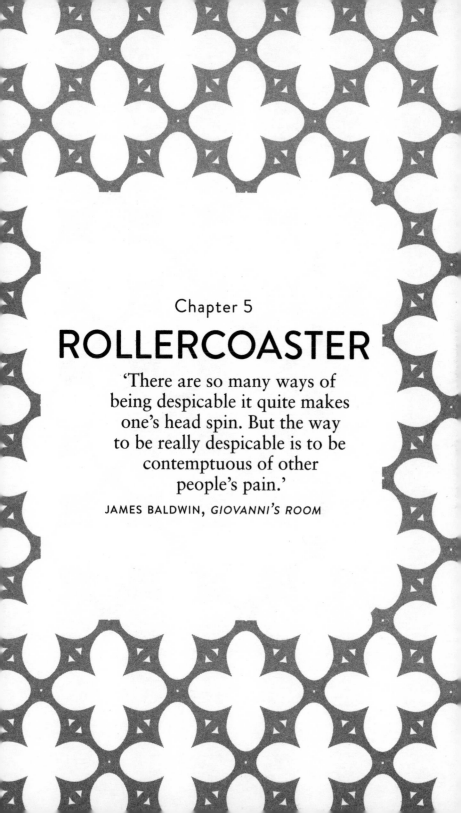

Chapter 5

ROLLERCOASTER

'There are so many ways of being despicable it quite makes one's head spin. But the way to be really despicable is to be contemptuous of other people's pain.'

JAMES BALDWIN, *GIOVANNI'S ROOM*

By the end of 2005, a rollercoaster of a year, I was back home in the care of my mother. I was really pleased to be back home. I'd had a very painful experience in the care system up to that point. Whatever problems I had previously had with my mother, it felt like home was where I should be. We would work it out like families do – together. For all her faults, my mother would never judge me for the colour of my skin or reject me because of my heritage. Being home felt like I could breathe again. I won't pretend that it was the very definition of domestic bliss, but the uneasy peace was holding quite well as my mother and I began to try again to build the relationship that had always eluded us.

I had returned to my old school, and something that resembled a normal routine began to emerge. Weeks went by and we prepared for a planned visit by the social work team. It was, and is, quite normal for social workers to call around to check up on how things are going. My mum had just popped out to a local shop to get some cakes and biscuits for the visit when our whole world was once again thrown into chaos.

There was a knock at the door, and I saw the outline of two people through the frosted glass. My siblings and I panicked as we realised it was the social workers arriving early for their visit and Mum wasn't back from the shop yet. We didn't answer the door and hoped they would just come back in a few minutes when Mum would be home. The next thing we knew, police officers were busting down the garden gate and coming into our sitting room via the conservatory. I guess something clicked in my head when I saw the social workers come in behind them. I realised that these people invading our home were there to take me and my siblings into care.

My siblings had never been in care, and I definitely didn't want them to go through everything I had just been through. They had been safe. Mum didn't hit them. She always did her best to look after them. It was me who was the problem child. It was me who wanted to rebel and deserved to suffer the consequences, not my siblings. I grabbed Solomon, shouted at Michael and Mary to follow me and ran up the stairs to my mum's room. We barricaded ourselves in the room and tried to hold them back for as long as we could – four children under 12, including an inconsolable three-year-old. They forced their way in eventually and dragged us downstairs one by one. As they were bringing me down, I saw that my siblings were effectively surrounded by social workers in the sitting room. In the chaos, I got loose and ran like I had never run before. There was a small field beside our house and I headed to a hidden area. There was a bush with a small hollow right under it, which meant that I could crawl into it in a matter of seconds and be practically unseen by passers-by.

I sat there, catching my breath and trying to come to terms with what had just happened and was still happening. Part of me was now regretting running and leaving my siblings behind, but I know that I had run out of sheer terror. Although I was horribly confused and curious about what might be going on back at the house, that same terror was keeping my butt firmly planted in that hedge. It was cold and the leaves I was sitting on were wet, but I couldn't motivate myself to crawl out. I stayed in there for what must have been an hour until my mother came and found me. She was distraught but relieved that she had found one of her children. She told me that the police had taken the other children and that she didn't know where they were.

She decided that she needed to get me away from there. She couldn't face losing me to the care system again, so she quickly made plans to take me to stay with an aunt in the UK. She said that once she had got me settled with my aunt, she would return to Ireland and fight to get her children back. It was such a crazy few days that I can't even remember how I felt about going to stay with my aunt, but I do know that I didn't want to go back into residential care. For her part, my mother needed space and to get away, even for just a couple of days. I think her plan was to reach out to our extended family for support, but once again she found that door slammed in her face. My aunt didn't immediately turn us away, but she made it clear that we couldn't stay for more than a couple of days. I can't say for sure if it was the frostiness of our welcome or the realisation that we couldn't simply run away that drove her back, but by the end of the fourth day away from Ireland we were heading back again.

We disembarked from the ferry in Belfast and boarded a bus back to Dublin. I don't think my mother had a clear plan of what to do next, but as it turned out, for the second time in less than a week, the police intervened and dictated proceedings. At some point during the journey, the bus pulled over to the side of the road and two guards got on. I didn't really understand why, but they were asking everyone for documents and checking them. When they got to my mum, they checked the documents she handed them. Then they asked us to come with them for a chat. We got off the bus and got into their marked Garda car. When we got to the station, my mum and I were taken into separate rooms. I was starting to get really scared and upset at this point. I kept asking if I could please just go be with my mum, but nobody would say anything to me or tell me what was going on.

Eventually, a police officer came into the room with my mum. The police officer told me I would have to go with him and Mum tried to console me as I started bawling my eyes out. I remember my mum telling me to 'just go with them' in a completely defeated tone of voice. It broke her to be without all four of her kids.

A duty social worker joined me and the police officer for the drive to my new home. I wasn't told where we were going but I feared the worst. I'd heard about care homes for naughty kids where they were locked in their room all day and had their bedsheets taken away if they didn't follow the rules. I didn't think I deserved to go somewhere like that for running away for a couple of days, but I had no idea what the rules of this terrifying new reality were. What if running away was enough to get put into one of those places? I remember crying uncontrollably for a while before gathering myself and reconciling myself to whatever would happen next.

As it turned out, I was being sent to Cork. I was placed in a residential care home with only plastic plates and forks so I couldn't self-harm. I was also not allowed to go anywhere without a social care worker at my side in case I tried to run away to be with my mum or my friends in Naas. Honestly, at that point I was too traumatised to even consider it.

*

I actually liked my new home in Cork. The social care workers and the other residents were nice. The only downside was that I couldn't go to school. There wasn't much time to get me into a new school before the new term started, and after it started it was even harder. After a few weeks of feeling like my brain cells were dying off, I begged my social worker to at least help me to source some form of home school. She was thankfully able to find me a home school tutor for maths and English.

My siblings were returned to my mum after a few weeks, and we got to have supervised visits in a coffee shop for a couple of hours every two weeks. During those visits, we felt like a real family, and I couldn't wait to be back home with them. Given my yo-yoing in and out of the care system over the previous few years, the social workers felt it was best to keep me in care for longer – about nine months longer. But eventually, I moved back in with my mum and the rest of my family for the last time.

*

I recently found out that mum had been suffering from a chronic pain condition that she had been struggling to get diagnosed with for over a decade. She was finally diagnosed with fibromyalgia. This is a condition that causes pain all over the body. Sometimes she would be in so much pain that she would need to walk with a cane and use a neck brace to get around. She seemed to be taking lots of different medications every day. I think some of them might have been to help with her mental health as well. My mum loved her kids, they meant the world to her. I know we had our issues but no mother wants her child to be taken from her. Me going into care impacted her already fragile mental health, but I think my siblings going into care was too much for her to handle. I don't think she had anyone to talk to or to support her during this time, and she became a shell of herself.

Mum got evicted from the house in Naas after she got my siblings back. She moved into a hostel in Cork so she could be close to my residential care home. But she had no friends who could help her out with looking after me and my siblings in Cork. After I was returned to her, she tried to get placed in a hostel in Dublin so that she could be closer to people who could help her out. When I think about it now, I wonder about how hard never being able to rest or feel settled was for her and how it impacted her condition.

We ended up sleeping on people's couches and floors for a bit before I was taken into care again. I don't know why this time, and I don't know why only I was taken, but I remember feeling a little relieved by the familiarity of the car ride to an unknown location that would have a bed and some heating.

There's a homeless hostel for young people in the heart of Dublin city. Most people probably don't even know it exists. If you've ever seen a play in the Abbey Theatre, been to the Laughter Lounge or waited for a bus or taxi on Eden Quay, you probably didn't realise that right there, on the corner of Marlborough Street, stands Lefroy House. This is where I was placed initially. During my first night there, I remember a social care worker explaining to me that some people were staying there who could pose a risk to me, so they had to lock me in my room to keep me safe while I slept. I can't put into words how terrifying that was to hear.

The next morning, I met Shelly from Focus Ireland. Shelly explained to me that I had to leave Lefroy House at 8 a.m. each day and that what I did with myself during the day was entirely up to me. Then in the evening I could call the homeless hostel and try to secure a bed for the night – but one was not guaranteed.

I had never lived in Dublin before, and I was terrified. I think Shelly sensed this, and she offered to let me sit in her office during the day so that I would at least be safe and warm. A bare office was hardly a dream scenario for a 13-year-old, but the lack of stimulation was not an issue. I was really grateful that someone took the time to care and to provide me with a little corner of safety and security. Who knows what might have happened to me if I had wandered the streets, what 'friends' I might have fallen in with, or worse. Shelly might not even remember me now, but I will never forget her or her kindness.

My time in Lefroy House lasted only a couple of nights. I then moved to Sherrard House, a girls-only homeless hostel. I stayed in the emergency bed there for a few weeks, making my usual trips with Shelly each morning. Initially, Shelly would try really hard to get me to chat with her, asking me questions to try to gauge my interest. She asked me what type of music I liked, who my favourite band were and what my favourite colour was. I provided some nice, polite responses but, honestly, I was still trying to get my head around what was going on, so I wasn't in the mood to talk about my top ten Busted songs. I felt like a freak for being in this situation, and I missed my friends. Eventually, a more stable bed opened up for me in Sherrard House, so I didn't have to leave each morning with everything I owned, anxious that I might not get to return to the same warm room and bed. But this 'stable' bed came with an expiration date. Anyone who moved in had to move out within three to six months. I ended up spending longer than six months in Sherrard House, but not by design.

I had started attending a local school shortly after moving into Sherrard House. While I was delighted to finally be attending a school, I wasn't in the best environment. During my time in Sherrard House, I was again subjected to some horrific racial abuse and bullying. I was assaulted by other residents, once seriously enough to require hospital treatment. On one occasion I even woke up to a fellow resident, who was about 15, standing over my bed, threatening to strangle me with a SCART lead.

School was a safe haven from my home life, but also a daily depressing reminder that my friends got to go home to loving families, while I went home to a place with bars on the windows. I wasn't always up for going, so Margaret, an education liaison worker assigned to work with me, set up a star chart system for me, with a bit of an extra incentive thrown in. In 2007, make-up for dark-skinned women was very hard to find in Ireland, and you could really only get it in places like Brown Thomas. In Brown Thomas, they had make-up counters where you could buy a make-up tutorial and spend the equivalent cost of the tutorial buying things from the make-up counter after it was over. I loved make-up, as many 13-year-old girls do, but obviously living in a homeless hostel meant that I couldn't afford to buy any from Brown Thomas.

So Margaret struck a deal with me. If I went to school every day for three months, I could get my make-up done at any counter in Brown Thomas and get a piece of my favourite make-up as a reward. It seems like something so small, but it meant the world to me that she made the effort to understand what would work best for me. She helped me to stay in school at a particularly turbulent time in my life, and I'm really thankful to her for that. While I was living in homeless hostels, Shelly and Margaret were definitely my biggest advocates. They took the time to try to understand me and to figure out what I needed and wanted. They saw that I wasn't just another kid in care. They made me feel hopeful.

*A letter to 13-year-old Debbie
in Sherrard House*

Debbie,

I want to give you the biggest hug. I wish you didn't have to go through the things you've gone through this year. I remember feeling like I wasn't sure I could handle any more bad things happening in my life. But the experience you've had in homeless hostels has just made you crave stability even more. You would love a normal home in a normal housing estate where you would feel safe. You are tired of all the moving around.

At some stage in the next few months, you will find a new home, and it will provide this normality that you are hoping for. Just hang in there.

Lots of love,
Your future self x

Chapter 6

HOME

'The function of freedom is
to free someone else.'

TONI MORRISON

My time in Sherrard House was coming to an end, and I hoped that something more settled was in the works, but I was going to wait and see before I got too excited. The way these things worked when moving to a new placement was that staff from the proposed home would visit you where you were living. If that went smoothly, without any issues sprouting up, then in the next stage you would go visit them. If that went okay, you were informed of the date you would be moving in.

My first contact with Dún na nÓg was with a man called Alan, who was introduced as the manager, and Lisa, who was introduced as one of the team leaders. Lisa seemed really nice. She was tall, with long black hair and blue eyes, and was a proud Galway girl. Alan had red hair, a beard and wore glasses – he also seemed bossy. He went straight into setting out house rules and expectations for each resident at Dún na nÓg. For example, smoking at 14 years old was frowned upon – which is kind of fair enough!

I liked pretty much everything about this proposed move. The house was lovely, and not that far from where I'd been living, so I could stay in the same school, and the staff I'd met seemed okay. I loved Lisa, and I had met the other team leader, Jenny, who also seemed nice and was very pretty. Perhaps most importantly, I had been introduced to the other two residents, and, because they didn't immediately greet me with a tirade of racially charged abuse, they had already managed to surge ahead of my previous housemates in my estimation. They seemed to really enjoy living there and even reassured me that once I got to know Alan and his strange sense of humour, I would find that he was actually quite nice.

They also explained that Alan had only just

taken over managing the house from another guy who had emigrated to Australia. Alan had been one of two deputies and had been promoted to manager, with the other leaving to manage a new house that the owners were opening down the road in Fairview. There was now a new, young team in Dún na nÓg. I even got to meet the owners of the house, who came in and welcomed me with a little gift. I can't remember exactly what it was, but this was the first time the proprietors of any house had come in specifically to welcome me. Their names were Paddy and Ciara. They were a couple and had children together. I didn't know it then, but I was meeting people who would play a major role in my life for years to come.

Let me explain what I mean when I say they were the 'owners' of a privately run residential home. Of the 187 care homes dotted around the country, some are state-run, which tend to be the larger institutions such as Oberstown and Ballydowd; some are voluntary homes, which traditionally have links to religious organisations; and some are privately owned care homes, the most recent phenomenon. A privately owned care home like Dún na nÓg is owned and run as a private company, which means that, in theory, it's run as a business. It would be easy to jump to conclusions here, like, 'Oh my God, are private companies cashing in on children in need?' But, in my experience at least, this was not the case. The reality is that there simply weren't enough homes available for the children who needed them, so some people, who in most cases had already worked in the field of social care, responded to that need by opening up privately owned care facilities. There is a rigorous registration process and, once accredited, the private care home becomes subject to exactly the same regulatory body, HIQA, as the state-run and voluntary services. The children themselves may never even know what type of home they are living in. As with most experiences in life, it is ultimately the people on the ground, not in the office, who make the difference.

My transition into Dún na nÓg continued and, after a few more visits, I officially moved in on 10 December 2007, which would prove to be an important date exactly one year on. Dún na nÓg was like Disneyland at the time. As with all houses, it's not the décor, but rather the people that turn a house into a home, and the signs were very good that, for the first time since I didn't know when, things would be okay.

Having quickly assimilated into life in Dún na nÓg, I became conscious that I was again living with two older girls, Jane and Aoife. My previous experience of this in the care home placement and in Sherrard House had been nothing short of horrific, so you can imagine that the presence of two older, much more streetwise girls was a potentially worrying scenario for me. My fears were quickly put to rest, though, as the atmosphere and culture of the house were far more inclusive. To their credit, Ciara, Paddy, Alan and the rest of the team worked hard to try to create a unified home. This was greatly helped by the warm welcome given to me by the two residents already living there.

Teenage girls don't always get along – bitchiness and jealousy can easily arise, particularly in the heightened atmosphere of a care home, when each girl has myriad issues going on in their own life. You couldn't help but feel that any type of domestic stability that was achieved in the home could be thrown into chaos by events happening elsewhere. It's not exactly a case of walking on eggshells, but when you live in care you become acutely aware that, regardless of how calm and settled the house might feel, bombs could be going off in the distance that could have serious ramifications for the residents, so over time you learn to tread softly and develop an awareness of potential triggers for others. 'Oh, great,' you might think, 'my mum is going to visit me soon.' While this might be great news for you, a loud announcement or outward excitement might inadvertently upset someone else. Such is the tightrope you walk when living in care, but walk it you must, and you learn to live with your mistakes.

For the most part, though, outside of some 'sibling rivalry', we really did get on great, particularly in those early days. We loved to socialise together, and we didn't need too much encouragement to get dressed up. One time, a dinner out in a fancy Dublin restaurant had been arranged for one of the girl's birthdays. Although the dinner was great fun, the biggest laugh we had was getting from the taxi to the restaurant. We got out of the taxi on Dame Street, only for us girls to find that we had to cling to Alan for dear life, as no one had warned us about the reality of walking on cobblestones in ridiculously high heels. Over the years I've had many great nights out in Temple Bar, but my first outing there taught me a valuable lesson: comfortable shoes are an absolute must. To the casual observer, the sight of a man in near hysterics of laughter visibly holding upright three disproportionately dressed-up teenagers wearing more make-up than a drag queen convention would have been quite a scene. Every perilous step brought forth further shrieks of terror, which did nothing to cure Alan of his giggling fit. The more he laughed, the more we screamed – mainly at him, I might add. (Did he not realise the physical danger and social embarrassment a fall might cause?) Alan took it all in his stride, and by the time we arrived at the restaurant, we had all joined him in his amusement. The terror of falling on my face was real, but looking back, these are the moments of unfettered joy that I remember from that time – a meal out, fancy clothes and a lot of laughs. From a distance, it might even have been considered normal.

Such happy events not only made us feel welcome and, to a degree, special – very few care homes go beyond the level of McDonald's or a weekly takeaway – they also brought us closer together. It's not rocket science that engaging in and celebrating important life events was a welcome distraction from our respective broken homes. Let's be honest about it, that's why children end up in care. It might seem like an oversimplification of the situation, but it's a helpful starting point. Each one of us had to be in care because our home situation had got to a point where it was no longer appropriate or safe to be there. It's a sad reality, but one that is at the heart of all our stories.

In Oberstown, where Alan had previously worked, the kids had been placed there by the courts as a result of criminal activity. Other children had been placed in secure accommodation (what we called 'lock-up') due to other forms of extreme or risk-taking behaviour. I'm not saying that these children didn't also come from difficult home situations or have equally sad stories, but the pathways to an open residential placement are different. We had not committed any crimes or broken any laws; we were there because our families were broken, or at least damaged enough that it was no longer acceptable for us to stay with them. We all knew it, but we also wished to hide it. The stigma of being in care is a crushing burden for a teenager already struggling with all the other ordinary pressures of that particular age bracket. We all wanted to appear as normal as possible. We all wanted to portray ourselves and our family situations as being 'not that bad, really'. We all lived with the duplicity of that reality in the knowledge that our external lives could come crashing down around us at any given moment. 'News from home' could often present an opportunity to 'front', but it's just as likely that it could bring us hurtling back to the pain of why we were there in the first place.

This desire to appear strong or in a better place than others – 'my family has problems, but at least my mum has a job' – is often a cause of conflict between residents. That might sound like an incredibly cruel thing to do, but it comes from a place of self-protection, a place of hurt. As the song by The Script goes, 'Hurt people, they hurt people'. The key understanding here comes from insight into why they do this. Hurt people don't intend to hurt others in a malevolent way, but rather are re-enacting the trauma that they have experienced in their relationship with others. My poor mother didn't set out to destroy our relationship or intentionally hurt me. She was the product of her own hurt and trauma, and quite simply did not have the tools to cope with and address that pain. Of course, I didn't know this at the time. It was all too close, too raw. Every day I was faced with the challenge of putting forward the bravest face I had – we all were. Ultimately, instead of driving us apart, it brought us girls from very different backgrounds closer together.

*

A number of social care workers at Dún na nÓg made a huge impact on my life, and I know they were genuinely working in my best interests. One in particular played an important role in my life at this time.

Debby is a beautiful Nigerian woman who worked in Dún na nÓg when I lived there, and who became a special part of my life for many reasons. It was a source of huge upset and shame for my mother that, when I was placed into care for the first time, there was nobody who could help me care for and maintain my hair. It might seem like something small, but where I came from, it was one of the rituals that helped forge the relationship between a mother and a daughter. I've since learned that, in many cultures, passing on personal grooming and beauty regimes is one of the most important rites of passage that children can learn from their parents. My mother and I had always bonded over such things. Debby was someone who not only looked like me but also understood the culture I'd come from. It was also reassuring for my mother to see a Black social care worker working in my care home. I think it was a genuine comfort to her that I had someone close to me who understood some of our cultural differences.

Debby deserved the title of Best Chef Ever. Debby is a skilled and multi-talented social care worker, and there are many aspects of her that I truly valued at the time and continue to value.

Having someone who came from the same tradition was unquestionably a huge plus to living in Dún na nÓg. This was a home where I had begun to feel settled and accepted, things I hadn't felt for a very long time. Little did I know that all that was about to change.

A letter to Debbie in Dún na nÓg

Debbie,

As you'd hoped, things have got better. I know you're worried about letting your guard down in case you end up having to move again. But try to be present and just enjoy the stability you had been hoping for. Ciara tries to ensure that every young person who lives in Dún na nÓg has as close to a normal upbringing as possible. She specifically went out of her way to recruit a Nigerian social care worker to work in the care home so you would feel more comfortable there. Even at 28, the people you met in Dún na nÓg are still an important part of your life. You've found your 'forever' home – or your 'until you turn 18' home, to be more accurate.

Lots of love,
Your future self x

Chapter 7

PREGNANT

'Choose people who lift you up.'

MICHELLE OBAMA

Jane and Aoife were both 16 when I moved in, and they felt like older sisters to me. We all had our own baggage, but we didn't really talk about that with each other. We talked about boys and make-up, normal things that teenage girls talk about. Both girls were dating boys from Wicklow, so we usually met them in Bray to hang out with them at the arcade.

As teenage relationships go, it wasn't always smooth sailing for Jane and her boyfriend. They often got into big fights and broke up, only for him to perform some big romantic gesture to get her back, which usually eventually worked. I was 14 and had never had a boyfriend. I was so jealous of their relationship, because even though it was clearly toxic, they cared a lot about each other, and I had never had anyone care about me that way.

Just after Christmas, Jane's boyfriend ended up in hospital. The three of us went to Wicklow to visit him there. When we arrived, she asked us to give them a few minutes alone. While we waited, one of Jane's ex-boyfriend's friends introduced himself to me. We got chatting, but I thought he was just being friendly.

When we got home, Jane got a text to say John wanted my number. 'Who's John?' I remarked, confused, given that we had just come from a hospital and not a house party. Aoife interjected to say he was the guy who had been flirting with me while we waited for Jane and her now-on-again boyfriend to talk. John was tall and had striking eyes. At the time I had a thing about falling for boys with really nice eyes. We ended up in a relationship that lasted for about four months.

After everything that had happened in my previous care home, I decided I wasn't having sex again until I had a boyfriend and had been with him for at least three months. That three-month mark fell at around the same time as Aoife's 17th birthday, when Aoife's boyfriend rented a house for the night so we could celebrate with her. I'm an introvert, so it used to be really hard for me to properly socialise around people I didn't know without at least a naggin of straight vodka in me. This night was no different. I got really, really drunk so I could enjoy the night. Then John and I snuck up to our room to celebrate our three-month anniversary. I would later find out that one of our condoms had broken while we were 'celebrating'.

Not long after that night, the rose-tinted glasses that I had viewed my relationship with John through had started to slip off. Our on-and-off relationship had been filled with drama, and I didn't know if all the heartache and tears were worth it anymore. I felt I deserved better, but I wasn't sure if it was just a bump in the road, so I didn't say anything to him.

About a week and half later, John came up to Dublin, so Aoife and I met up with him. Jane had moved out soon after I met John. She had been put in a care home in the UK. We hated being apart from her.

At one point, Aoife was talking to John about trying to have a baby with her boyfriend. She said she thought she might finally be pregnant, and then John jokingly said, 'Sure, Debbie could be pregnant too!' I stopped walking and asked him what he was talking about. He confessed that the condom had, in fact, broken, and he didn't tell me because he didn't want me to take the morning-after pill.

Aoife and I went home and asked the social care workers for a pregnancy test. They knew Aoife was trying to get pregnant, so she said it was for her. We went into her room to take the test. The instructions stated that if I was pregnant, two lines would show up. It had been less than two weeks since I had had sex, so we weren't sure if the test could even work so early.

I took the test, and the first line showed up clearly, and then a faint second line started appearing. It stayed faint, so I decided that meant I wasn't pregnant. Aoife then opened a drawer full of used pregnancy tests to show me how none of her negative tests had a second faint line. She convinced me that we needed to do a second test, but I made her swear not to say anything to our social care workers about how the first test had turned out. She went out of the room to ask them for a second test while I sat on her bed trying to stop myself from thinking that I might be pregnant at 14 years old.

I guess Aoife didn't usually ask for a second test, so this set off alarm bells with the social care workers that someone might be pregnant. They got her the test, but we refused to tell them how the first one went. I took the second test, and the result was the same – a second faint line. Then Alan knocked on Aoife's door and asked if it was safe to come in. We hid the tests and I made her swear not to say anything. I didn't have a plan, but I knew that the sooner I told them the sooner I would have to move out. I'd finally settled somewhere, but I had messed it up massively! I needed time to make a plan.

Alan then came in and sat on the floor of Aoife's bedroom. At first, nobody spoke. Eventually, not meeting anybody's eyes, Alan asked, 'So, does somebody want to tell me who's pregnant?'

*

After a turbulent few years, I had at last reached a place of stability and, all things being relative, security. I loved the house, and although things were by no means perfect, I was feeling pretty good and was just about daring to start being a teenager again. Yes, I was in care. Yes, I'd had enough physical and emotional turmoil to last a lifetime. But at that moment, I had a nice place to live, complete with a manager who, although he could be a bit of a headwrecker, genuinely seemed to care about me. I had only been living in Dún na nÓg for a couple of months, but I had been attending the same school in Drumcondra for nearly a year and had a great group of friends outside my care home. Compared to what I had come from, life was now much more stable, and I welcomed the respite. Of course, if I had seen myself as a character in a dramatic story, I would have realised that the challenges I had previously faced were merely a prelude to the ones that lay ahead.

I didn't consciously let my guard down. I just wanted to have some normal teenage experiences and, who knows, possibly some fun. It's easy to look back and castigate myself for errors of judgement or things that I could have done differently, but when I remember that I was 14, living in care, and had had the experiences that I'd had in the previous few years, I can't judge myself too harshly. I was making my own choices, fighting my corner when I needed to and generally trying to get on with just living my life and being myself.

*

The image of Alan sitting in the middle of my bedroom floor asking which one of us was pregnant is the one that stays with me the most. In one way it's a poignant reminder of the humanity of care workers, who are themselves subject to doubt, indecision and the full spectrum of emotions that accompany any similar life situation. But it's also a reminder of the panic I was starting to feel. Children in care often regard staff as, if not all-knowing, at least authoritative figures who are well-trained in the art of crisis management, and who, no matter how annoying they can be, will offer some sort of practical solution to the crisis at hand. At that particular moment, however, Alan just looked like a man sitting on a bedroom floor wondering what to do next. I know now that, although Alan was an experienced care professional, he had spent most of his career working predominantly with teenage boys, including five years working in juvenile detention. During that time he dealt with many extremely difficult and, at times, violent crises. What he hadn't encountered was one of his charges potentially being pregnant. I use the term 'potentially' here, as at this point we were still in the realm of the unknown. That's why the image of Alan sitting there still brings a smile to my face. The reality of the situation had yet to unfurl, so having the manager of the home sitting there, caught off-guard, was pretty funny. Alan always had a way of bringing humour and a few laughs (whether he meant to or not) to every situation. As it turned out, the laugh barrel would run fairly dry in the weeks and months that followed.

The fact was that I was in total denial. 'There's no way that I'm pregnant. I simply couldn't be pregnant. It's such a faint line – how reliable are these home tests anyway?' As if to echo these thoughts, Alan, having recovered his practical sensibilities, suggested a trip to a local GP. His rationale was that we needed to know for sure before we started to develop a plan, whereas I was still resistant ('I can't be pregnant, it will ruin everything!') and really didn't want to go.

I think we all hoped that the doctor would reassure us that we could all return to our normal lives. At times like this, we hope to meet the doctor we've all seen in films, a kindly old man complete with a white coat and stethoscope, filled with warmth and uncondescending authority. But the doctor we went to wasn't wearing a white coat or a stethoscope. He looked reasonably smart, but lacked any real warmth, and didn't appear particularly interested in providing the reassurance we so desperately sought. He brusquely told us that he would provide a similar test to the one I'd already done. When he confirmed the result, reality finally started to take hold. You can't be a little bit pregnant – you're either pregnant or you're not. Alan, always wanting to be reassuring, had at least outwardly decided to use the information learned in the GP's office to start making plans. 'Well, that's that, I suppose,' he said.

Getting pregnant in care at the time meant you had to move into a state-run mother and baby home. I didn't know much about them, but I'd heard from others in care that these homes weren't supportive, and that the social care workers there took your baby away if you messed up just one time. I was filled with anxiety about what would happen next, but given the clusterfuck my life had been in the previous three years, I wasn't optimistic this was going to end well.

I can look back now and say my pregnancy was the catalyst for me to become everything I am now. But at that moment, at 14 years old, with the news that I'd just received still sinking in, everything I had grown to trust was now in question: my home, my education, my prospects, my relationship with my family.

Looking back, it's impossible to separate all the emotions and fears into different departments. It wasn't just one thing, but rather all of it that kept hitting me, wave after wave. One of the most immediate terrors, though, was the impending physical trauma of childbirth itself. I had a 14-year-old's body, and the thought that a potentially large baby was going to (a) grow inside of me and (b) at some point want to get out was utterly terrifying. These feelings had far less to do with worrying about what would happen to my figure and far more to do with the concept that there was only one available exit – and that it was going to hurt like hell.

It's funny when I think of it now, but I really was terrified. When you're a teenager, you tend to have a confidence that doesn't match your actual life experience. You have a sense that you're all grown up and can handle anything. The reality of a teenage pregnancy can bring that perception crashing down in a hurry. When your body is going to start doing very adult things, you really do grow up in a hurry. You have to.

Telling your parents that you're pregnant when you're 14 isn't easy for any girl, but the fact that my parents were estranged meant that I had to have that conversation twice. I was far more nervous about telling my father, because, apart from everything else, he was the shepherd (which was like a pastor) of his own church – a church with very strict conservative values regarding moral conduct, and one that would take a dim view of pregnancy outside of wedlock. I had seen my father's reaction to similar situations, and knew that it wasn't going to be an easy conversation. As it turned out, after the initial shock, he took it rather well and ended up being very supportive. This was a major relief, as I'd considered the prospect of being disowned to be a real possibility. I was reassured by his reaction, and I thought that I had cleared the more difficult of the two parental hurdles. I hadn't.

To say that my mother wasn't pleased would be an understatement. Thinking back, I can imagine what would have been going on in her mind. It would have been filled with the guilt of letting me down by being taken into care or letting the family back in Nigeria down by allowing this to happen. But she was raging. In fact, she initially barred me from seeing my other siblings for about a month. My mother was worried that if my siblings knew, they would let the cat out of the bag by saying it to others. I knew that she would be upset, but I had hoped for a little more understanding. The fact that she was so angry with me was both hurtful and a little surprising, at least in the context that I had expected the real fire and brimstone from my father, not her.

However, her attitude soon took a surprising turn for the better, which came as a huge boost at a time when the reality of the situation was really starting to sink in. To understand her change of heart, you have to understand the wider immigration landscape at the time in Ireland – something I had no insight into myself nor the time to worry about. Without getting bogged down in it, there were things to do with residency applications that were made easier when you had a child who was born to an Irish parent. Whether or not my situation directly helped her is still unclear, but once she found out that my baby had an Irish father, her perception of the situation changed dramatically. My unborn child went from being a pariah to all of a sudden being a blessing, a gift from God that she saw as offering her and her children a renewed sense of hope for the future.

Although her change of heart was a great encouragement to me, I certainly didn't share her sense of optimism. After all, I had been in the care system for the past few years and was less than enthused by how this latest development could be seen as a positive for me. Far from it. The new sense of security that I had begun to get used to since my arrival in Dún na nÓg was now under threat, and my growing understanding of the situation held very few advantages. I would lose my home, I would lose my child, and my future prospects in terms of my education and career seemed equally dim. I was 14 and in care. My family was fragmented, and now I was pregnant. To say that my future looked uncertain doesn't do the situation justice.

To use an accounting metaphor, there was a disproportionate amount of red in my ledger, and statistics for the future prospects for young Black pregnant girls in care would not have provided me with any comfort. Things looked extremely bleak, and at the time I couldn't see what I had going for me. But I had something that I neither was aware of nor could possibly imagine would prove so valuable: people who believed in me.

*

'If you had the baby now, it would be taken away from you.'

Those were the exact words spoken to me by my social worker in the very first conversation I had with her following the news that I was pregnant. I should point out that they weren't the first words she said, but, when pressed on what might happen with regard to long-term planning, that was her response. I suppose, in some sense, she was just trying to be honest. Although it was a little blunter than I was prepared for, it did help to show me the seriousness of my situation.

All my initial fears were about the fact that I could lose my new home and have to go live in some form of state-run mother and baby home. The prospect of having to move out and once again be surrounded by judgemental strangers had haunted me ever since the penny had dropped, but up until this conversation with my social worker, it hadn't occurred to me that my baby would be taken from me. Why would it? Had I already done something wrong to prove that I would be a bad mother? I was very young, that's for sure, but after spending the last number of years in the social care system, I felt like I'd had to grow up in a hurry. I'm not trying to say that I was fully matured or anything like that, but I was already starting to feel a connection to the life growing inside me, and the thought that we would be separated cut right to the core of my being. Letters and reports were going back and forth about my ability to cope. It was hard enough to find my own footing in the world after all that had happened, but now would I have to fight for my baby too?

When I told John I was pregnant, he was over the moon. He told his mum and, apparently, she agreed to let me move in with them. John assured me he would help with the baby while I went to school if I moved in with him. I had grown very bored of John's empty promises at this stage, and never seriously considered the offer. He wasn't reliable on a good day, so what would he be like with a screaming baby in the middle of the night? I assured him that he could play as much or as little of a role in our baby's life as he wanted once he or she was born. He isn't a bad guy; he just wasn't the guy for me.

Teenage pregnancy is hardly unusual, but when it happens in a situation such as mine, you can only imagine the shitstorm that accompanies it. There was no proper template for it, and what was going to happen next was up in the air. Social care workers are trained to deal with crises, and one of the first questions they are meant to ask when one occurs is, 'What does the young person need or want?' It seems like a fairly straightforward question, but it's based on the theory that feelings are behaviour and behaviour is feelings. In other words, a young person is acting a certain way because they are feeling a certain way. So by establishing what they need or want, you can also establish a course of action to address it.

In this case, however, I didn't know what I wanted or what the solution would look like, other than I wanted not to be pregnant. And there's the rub. Pregnancy is a definitive state. You are either pregnant or not pregnant. If you are pregnant and want a baby, then you have completed stage one and are through to the next round. If you are pregnant and don't want to be pregnant, the choices (and 'choice' here becomes a highly politicised word) become a lot more stark. If you don't want to be pregnant and you want to take steps to address that situation, then you are going to encounter another word that has absolutely no ambiguity in the political sphere: abortion.

There is a very important distinction between the anxiety (at times downright terror) that I was experiencing – wanting it all to go away, wishing that I had never become pregnant – and actually seeking to end it. I am pro-choice, but recognising someone else's right to have an abortion and even fighting for that right does not necessarily mean that you want one yourself.

My first meeting with Sherie de Burgh took place in the offices of One Family just off Baggot Street in Dublin. One Family is a charity that offers counselling and support services to single parents. They've moved from there now, but back then their office was in one of those Georgian buildings that graces that part of Dublin. I sat down in the small reception area and waited to be called. After a short time, a woman with cropped brown hair and a fringe came out and called me in. I felt a sense of genuine welcome and ease about this woman.

She had greeted me with such a broad smile and had the kindest brown eyes I had ever seen. I was immediately disarmed and felt completely comfortable in her presence. Nothing that happened in the next hour would do anything to alter this first impression. The thing that stuck with me the most upon meeting her was her apparent lack of agenda or ulterior motive. Here was someone who just wanted to chat and, even more importantly, to listen.

Throughout my journey through care, I encountered many people whom I found it very difficult to relax around because I knew that they had some sort of pre-existing agenda or, even worse, had already made up their minds about me. Yet here was someone who gave the instant impression that she was just going to be there for me. Me as a person, not as a problem or as a case to be resolved. Me. No pretext, no judgement, just compassion and support. Of course, I didn't find all that out in that first hour, and perhaps with the passage of time I'm overestimating how positive that first meeting was, but I can truly say that I left her office that day feeling affirmed and validated as a person.

At a time when I was very much in need of people on my side, it felt like my circle of allies had grown.

*

This period of my life was so momentous, so unsettling and yet so defining that it's difficult to pick out any specific moment or catalyst that centred me, guided me towards a specific course of action or reassured me that things were going to work out and that it would all be okay. The cloud of uncertainty that had consumed my every thought and action since I had learned that I was pregnant wasn't going to be dispersed by one event or conversation, or by the repetitive reassurance of care staff. Not because any of it was unwelcome or ill-intentioned – far from it. I always appreciated when people took the time to talk things through and calm me down, but ... talk is cheap. It would take significant and meaningful action to persuade me that my immediate to medium-term future (and that of my unborn child) was in any way secure.

No single event could do this, but one certainly helped. I remember this particular day being warm,

as I had been sitting outside in the back garden.
I also remember it was a Wednesday, because
the weekly staff meeting had been on, and after
it finished I had gone up to talk to Alan about
something in the sitting room. We spoke for a few
minutes before he said he had something to do in
the office and left me in the sitting room. I immediately noticed that he had left my care plan book
on the couch where he'd been sitting. Every young
person living in the home had a care plan book –
indeed, every young person had an entire drawer
in the filing cabinet in the office that contained
anything and everything to do with your life, from
copies of your birth certificate and passport to
placement reports and your medical history. The
care plan book, however, was more like a day-
to-day book that contained reports on your daily
activities, medication given, contact information,
etc. Apparently, at any time, a young person can
request to read this book or see anything in their
own file, but I certainly didn't know this.

Immediately after Alan left the room, I closed
the sitting-room door and began reading. I had
seen the book before, so much of it came as no

great revelation to me. The bit I really wanted to get to was the 'daily report' section, which was filled out every day, morning and evening, by the staff on duty, and gave an account of any significant (and frequently insignificant) events or occurrences in the young person's life. A typical entry might read something like, 'Debbie was called by staff at 9 a.m. She then got up and made herself breakfast before returning to her room for an hour. She accompanied staff to the local shop for grocery shopping before returning and preparing lunch.' Riveting stuff, I know, but it was meant to be a factual account of events. Occasionally I could feel the personality of different staff members coming through in the writing style or through the different relationships I had with each of them. The writing was meant to be unopinionated reporting, but it's almost impossible to avoid some level of subjectivity when you are personally involved.

As I leafed through the entries, I came across a rather lengthy entry that Alan had recently added. It wasn't normal for Alan to make entries in my daily section, as that was usually done by the care staff each day, but I knew it was his writing straight away as it was quite distinctive. I noticed that it had been written within the last week and that it detailed correspondence between Alan and the house owners, Ciara and Paddy. While I didn't know Ciara and Paddy well (but I would get to know them a lot more in the coming months and years), the fact that I knew them at all was a marked difference from the other houses I had lived in. Not only had they stopped by to welcome me when I moved in, but I saw them from time to time when they called in to talk to Alan or deal with issues around the house. Paddy frequently carried out repairs or maintenance in the house and garden himself. My point is that I knew who they were, and they were central to any major plans or initiatives about the running of the home.

I say all this for context, because what Alan's entry detailed was a relatively embryonic proposal to develop Dún na nÓg from a mainstream residential home into a home that could cater for young people in care who can live with their babies. I use the term 'embryonic' deliberately, not just for the obvious pun, but also to indicate that the suggestion was light on specific details of how this might happen. However, what it lacked in detail, it more than made up for in heart. It asked a very basic question, one that will resonate with me for the rest of my life: 'Why should Debbie lose her home simply because she has become pregnant?'

He went on to talk about how Aoife would be moving in with her boyfriend soon (sometimes kids in care get to move into 'independent living' in their own apartment before they turn 18 if they are deemed mature enough), how much he and his staff had invested in me and that, although he had no idea how it might all work, he proposed that we commit to working with me through the pregnancy and continue to provide a home and support for me after my baby was born.

From my conversations with Alan, I knew that the prospect of me having to move out was both-ering him quite a bit, but I had no idea that he was going to propose taking the home in a whole new direction simply for my benefit. To see those words written down was like a beam of light and warmth entering my soul. This really meant something.

Although I was surprised and delighted in equal measure, the significance of what was going to happen didn't really sink in for some time. To this day, I don't know whether or not Alan deliberately left the book there for me to read. When I asked him about it years later, he just smiled at me and winked. What I did know was that this was a very positive development. In the midst of the maelstrom, somebody had cared enough to do something genuine to help. Maybe, just maybe, I was ready to accept it.

*

Everything had been organised, agreed and signed off on for the new Dún na nÓg mother and baby home. My mum wasn't living in a secure housing situation at the time, so she was thankful I would have somewhere safe to live with my newborn baby. It was a very exciting time. Although there was still a lot of stress and anxiety, there were a lot of pleasant distractions too. Ciara has done, and continues to do, so much that I will be eternally grateful for, but as I was only just getting to know her properly at this time, my fondest memory of her is that it was she who got me, and kept me, excited about my pregnancy. The first thing I learned about Ciara is that pregnancy, babies and everything that goes with them are her favourite things in the world. I'm not saying that she wasn't interested in the care home before I got pregnant – far from it – but it was as though she found her groove when she started working closely with me.

Ciara's mother, Mary, who I also know and still have a great relationship with, set up and has run care homes in the UK and in Ireland for many years and Ciara followed in her footsteps. Dún na nÓg in Drumcondra was the first home they opened (about five years before I moved in), and over that time it had been finding its feet and establishing itself as a highly thought-of residential home. I know this because my social worker at the time hadn't even tried to hide her delight that they had decided to accept my referral, as she had heard 'only good things' about the home in Drumcondra. With a solid reputation established, it must have been quite a daunting prospect to revamp their entire service, but I can't help but think that Ciara's eyes must have lit up when she read Alan's letter.

In fact, I'm not entirely certain that she hadn't already been thinking something similar. I'd been worried that Alan's suggestion might not have been met with the same level of enthusiasm at their end, but my fears were quickly put to rest when Ciara showed up about a week later with a pile of catalogues and assorted second-hand baby items.

At that point, Ciara was way more excited than I was, but her positivity and energy were infectious, and it really cheered me up. I quickly learned that we also shared a passion for shopping. I was delighted with the second-hand stuff that she had given me, but she also stressed how eager she was to supply me with new things that would be special for me and my baby. I can remember a few eyebrows being raised at the price of the Moses basket that she ordered, and I know that at times she and Paddy went deep into their own pockets to ensure that both I and this new service had the very best of everything.

It wouldn't be the last time that they would go above and beyond in terms of statutory require-ments, but it wasn't just about the expense they went to. For the first time, they made me feel that being pregnant and becoming a mother could be a positive development in my life. Before Ciara came on the scene, the word that I most associated with what was happening was 'crisis', and I understand why, but it was also starting to feel like an opportunity. An opportunity for what exactly still wasn't clear, but I no longer felt completely alone. I no longer felt the tug of that rug under my feet, but rather, with every passing day I felt a little bit more at home, something I hadn't felt for a long time.

A letter to pregnant Debbie

Debbie,

I wish I could go back and tell 14-year-old me that everything is going to be okay. My biggest worries were how I would cope with a baby, if John would be present in the baby's life, how painful labour was going to be and how many stretch marks I was going to get. Ciara, in particular, helped me to deal with a lot of those worries. For example, she got me loads of parenting books so I could learn how to cope with a baby. She also got me oils and creams to help prevent stretch marks. I don't know why she bothered. She always went above and beyond for the kids in her care home. I am so thankful to her for this because she really tried to help me to enjoy my pregnancy. She was one of the few people who didn't make me feel like being pregnant so young was something I needed to feel permanently ashamed about. Don't worry, you aren't going to have to go through this all alone, and everything is going to be okay.

Lots of love,
Your future self x

Chapter 8

BECOMING A MOTHER AND LOSING MINE

'Although the world is full of
suffering, it is full also of the
overcoming of it.'

HELEN KELLER

My pregnancy was horrific. I suffered from hyperemesis gravidarum, which causes severe vomiting during pregnancy. I couldn't drink a glass of water in the morning without it coming back up soon after. The only thing I could actually keep down was beef strips and rice with salt and lashings of chilli powder. Unfortunately, this meant I was unusually thin during my pregnancy.

My due date was on 23 December 2008. My dad arrived two weeks earlier to support me after the baby was born, and to visit my siblings. My little sister Mary's birthday was on 8 December and, because my dad had flown in on that date, we decided to celebrate with a family dinner on 9 December. I saved up my pocket money so I could treat us both to getting our make-up done before dinner as my present to her. Before the make-up appointment, I had one of my regular check-up appointments in the Rotunda Maternity Hospital.

I had hoped to be in and out quickly, so I was shocked when the doctor told me that he was concerned about the baby's weight and that he felt more comfortable inducing the birth that day. Firstly, I didn't know what 'inducing' meant, because I had been scared to engage with any books or information about how the actual birth would work. I just knew there were drugs to remove the pain – and I wanted those drugs. The rest could be a surprise.

On 10 December 2008, my son Liam Callum Joshua was born in the Rotunda Hospital in Dublin. Although John and I were no longer together, I didn't have to go through the process on my own. I had a doula called Leemore with me the whole time. Quite early on in my pregnancy, Ciara had proposed the idea of having a doula to help and advise me. Needless to say, I had never heard of such a thing, but when it came to pregnancy, I decided to trust Ciara, and in this matter she did not disappoint. A doula is a professional, non-medical companion trained in the needs of the family. They provide clients with continuous support during pregnancy, labour and birth, as well as in the post-partum period.

The birthing process wasn't like a scene from a horror movie, as I had imagined it would be. I got an epidural as soon as I was allowed to get one. With three pushes, Liam was here. I can't explain it, but I felt an overwhelming feeling of love for Liam the minute I saw him. The arrival of my new baby would be a catalyst for many changes in my life, but at that moment, like every new parent, I was just relieved that everything had gone according to plan and that the correct number of fingers and toes were present.

Alan was at my bedside when I woke up, feeding Liam. I had fallen asleep when they wheeled me to the ward, but he and Leemore decided not to wake me as I had been up all night in labour. This was just the type of really thoughtful stuff Alan did. My parents and siblings were waiting downstairs and came up to visit me when they heard

I was awake. Up to this point, my dad had been really cool and progressive about the whole teenage daughter getting pregnant scenario. But he was furious when he saw bottled formula on the table beside my bed. He said that if I gave my baby that, instead of breastfeeding him, he would have brain damage. I honestly couldn't believe how archaic what he was saying was.

Then my mum did something I didn't expect – she took my side. She explained to my dad that things had changed, and that formula contains the same nutrients as breast milk. As a 15-year-old, I don't know what weirded me out more – the thought of breastfeeding or my parents standing there debating whether I would breastfeed. In the end, I guess my mom and I won, because he calmed down and came around to the idea. When I first got pregnant, the idea that my mum, dad and siblings would all be sitting around my hospital bed happily staring at my baby wasn't something that had even crossed my mind as a possible reality. But here we were. Everyone wanted a turn holding him, and my mum was on hand to help me with anything I needed.

Strangely, it wasn't until I had a child of my own that we finally found a way to get along, but moving back in with her wasn't an option at this stage. I was under a full care order, meaning that the state was my legal guardian and dictated where I lived. My mum and siblings were still living in a cramped one-bed hostel room and certainly didn't have room for me and my baby. I guess my mum at this time was thankful I was in care and had the right support around me to help me to look after my baby, but she still made sure she was there for me if I needed her. That meant so much to me. Although it was utterly exhausting, I remember those next few weeks as a whirlwind of continuous excitement and discovery. The anxiety – and at times blind terror – that I had experienced were now replaced with more and more moments of joy.

Liam had brought my family together for the first time in a long time. My parents were speaking again, and we were about to be united for Christmas, all of us together. That Christmas turned out to be one of the most enjoyable in my memory. As you might imagine, Christmastime in a residential care home could be a mix of many different emotions, but that year, with the arrival of Liam, the conflicting nature of my situation seemed to melt away for those few weeks. In social care, particularly at Christmas, every effort is made to facilitate some form of family reunification on and around Christmas Day. Because there were no other young people in the care home on Christmas Day, my family was free to visit and spend the whole day celebrating Christmas together.

Alan set about preparing one of the most amazing Christmas dinners. He pulled out all the stops: turkey, ham, two types of potatoes, loads of veg and his signature chilli chutney, which I absolutely adored. Every year, I am honoured to receive a fresh batch of it just in time for Christmas. It was a magical day, and by the time everyone left they were all suitably stuffed and happy. I'm so glad that Alan remembered to take pictures that day, which I still have. Neither the day nor the situation was perfect, but in some ways, it was something even more important than perfect. It was precious.

Due to the reality of having separate but related religious traditions, Liam actually underwent two baptismal ceremonies. One, hastily arranged only a week after the birth, in keeping with my father's wishes, saw me sitting in a separate room at the back of a church in Blanchardstown. The reason that the mother is removed from the ceremony is that she's still bleeding after giving birth, and women who are bleeding, even during their period, aren't allowed to enter the church. At the time, I was neither warned what would happen nor had I the energy to object. I went along with it because it made my dad happy, and that was important to me at the time. The second ceremony, a Catholic baptism, happened a few months later. I had made my communion and confirmation while in school in Naas, so I wanted Liam to be baptised in this tradition.

In order for me to keep living in Dún na nÓg, an agreement was reached that I would need to undergo a daily evaluation of my fitness to be a mother. A very thorough evaluation form was developed by my social worker, which placed me under a microscope during my first three months as a mother. I didn't feel like this daily evaluation was put in place to support me as a new mum.

Honestly, it felt like I was being handed a long list of ways I could fuck up and have my kid taken away from me. I didn't feel like my social worker had much faith in my ability to actually successfully complete the three-month evaluation. My anxiety about this test of perfection to keep my baby was like a dark cloud that followed me around during my pregnancy. Eventually, I decided I had to try to take control of the situation. I was determined to prove that I was the best person on the planet to look after my little boy.

While reading books about delivering a baby was a big no-no during my pregnancy, reading books about what happens after the baby was born was something I was obsessed with. I had chosen and documented a routine for Liam before he was even born. I wanted to do everything myself for the first few weeks. Dún na nÓg offered support with babysitting hours to help me get some sleep during the day, but I felt that if I had accepted this it would have been a sign of failure, or that I couldn't cope. However, Sherie helped me to understand that a new mum at any age needed help. In the end, I accepted the help.

While my mum and I were now getting along better, her mental health had started to decline sharply. I didn't realise how bad things had become until I got a call to say my mum had attempted suicide. She had taken an overdose with prescribed medication, and my brother had found her lying on her bed unconscious in the one room all four of them shared at the direct provision hostel that they were living in. This is an image that still haunts him, especially as he was the closest to my mum. My siblings were taken into care again until my mum could get better.

She was then granted asylum and had to move out of the direct provision hostel into accommodation for people experiencing homelessness. She had nowhere to go and had no fight left in her. I wasn't aware of the signs of depression, and I certainly didn't know that was what my mum was going through. She would come to the care home and spend the day with my son while I was in school, but she came because she had nowhere else to go. I hoped that at least spending time with Liam would help to cheer her up.

About a month later, she walked into the sea

on Dollymount Strand with fistfuls of rocks in her pockets, only to be pulled out and brought to a hospital by ambulance. When I visited her at the hospital, the nurse told me she was just faking it, and that she was perfectly fine. She was discharged within a few hours and without a proper follow-up. I didn't believe the nurse that my mum had been faking it, but I couldn't force them to keep her in the hospital. She came home with me and took a nap on my bed. When I went to wake her, I saw her without a hat on for the first time in a while – my mum, who had long, beautiful hair that I was always so jealous of, had shaved all her hair off. This really shocked me, but I tried to hold it together until she left. I didn't want the care workers in Dún na nÓg to think my mum's visits were upsetting me and put a stop to them, so I headed to bed early with Liam and cried as quietly as I could into my pillow. I didn't know what to do, or how to help.

The next morning I decided to take a more proactive role in bringing my mum to her appointments and trying to help her secure accommodation for herself and my siblings so that she could start working towards getting them back. Going to those appointments and seeing how disengaged and withdrawn she was had been heartbreaking. But I kept telling myself that once we got her a place and the kids were back with her everything would be okay.

Unfortunately, everything wasn't okay. My mum was tired of fighting, and she just wanted to be at peace. My mother, Princess Oriyomi Somorin, died on 17 September 2009, after taking an overdose of prescribed medication. Suicide marks an end for the person who commits it, but for those left behind, the pain and confusion can go beyond measure. The greatest pain I still feel to this day regarding the loss of my mother is the fact that I can't go to her for advice or reassurance. Losing my mother at such an early stage of my own parenting journey was devastating to me. It still is. Every time I think of her or talk about her, I start crying.

I know we would have a much better relationship if she was here today. She would finally be proud of me and I would be more understanding of her. Wherever she is, I hope she's happy, and I hope she's able to check in on me and my siblings.

We meant the world to her, and I know that deciding to leave us was the hardest decision that she ever had to make. That's why I cry when I think of her. I just imagine the immense pain she must have been in to think her children would somehow be better off without her. We weren't. We needed her. We still do.

A letter to Debbie after Mum's passing

Debbie,

I know this feels like a bad dream. It's hard to accept that your mum is really gone. You don't understand how she could leave you and your siblings all alone because you could never do that to Liam. But, you'll come to understand that she didn't do this because she was choosing to leave you and your siblings alone. She was suffering from depression, and this was the only way she felt she could find peace at the time. I wish she had held on, but for reasons only she knows, she decided this was her time. I know it feels like you're never going to be okay again after this. It feels like a part of you was just ripped away and you'll never be whole again. But I promise that, over time, you'll learn to live with this sadness. You'll find ways to keep her memory alive by sharing stories with your siblings and supporting each other.

Lots of love,
Your future self x

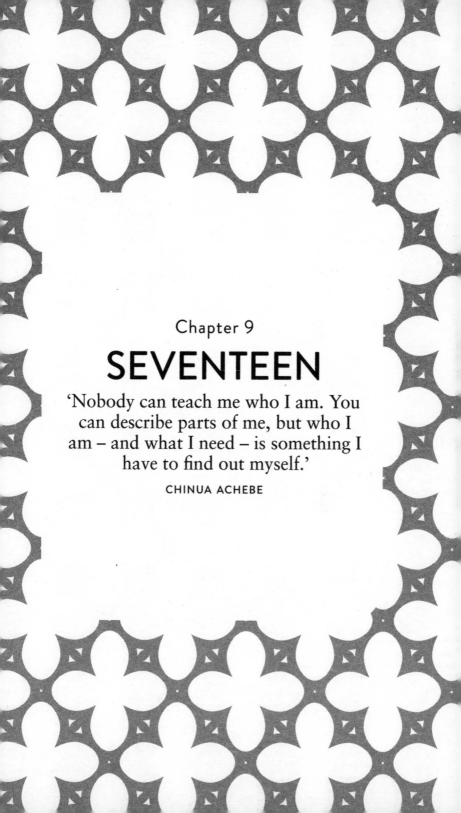

Chapter 9

SEVENTEEN

'Nobody can teach me who I am. You can describe parts of me, but who I am – and what I need – is something I have to find out myself.'

CHINUA ACHEBE

After my mum passed away, I got really depressed. I just had this overwhelming feeling that I was all alone in this world. My dad hoped that a trip to Nigeria, to spend time with my mum's family in particular, would help me to feel less lonely. He planned a trip for me and Liam during the summer of 2010. Even with my dad financing the trip, the amount of bureaucracy and number of hoops that had to be jumped through to ensure that it could happen were incredible. I remember picking up Liam's passport, and the lady at the counter remarking in a slightly alarmed tone, 'You're a baby travelling with a baby!'

This was my first trip back to Lagos since I was 10 years old, so it was also my first time back in my old house again. I was quite taken aback to find that all our rooms had remained almost completely untouched since we'd left them over seven years before. A mural with my favourite cartoons was still on my bedroom wall, and the clothes I hadn't taken with me still hung in the closet. Even some of my mother's things were still there and, since her death, my father had had several large pictures of her framed and hung on the walls in prominent locations. It felt as if the ghost of not only my mother but the ghosts of all of our past lives together wafted through the entire house. While I was delighted to be back home visiting, there was an inescapable sense of sadness that pervaded the rooms. It was obvious to me not only how hard the passing of my mother had hit my father, but that perhaps informing this grief was the stark reality that he had never truly recovered from her leaving.

I'm sure some would judge my father harshly for the mistakes he made around his family, and while I understand why some would take a critical stance, I don't. The question has been raised with me on several occasions as to why he didn't scoop us all up and take us back to Nigeria, particularly when things really started to go wrong for us as a result of my mother's mental health. It's a perfectly valid question, but there were so many layers of complexity to the situation that it never became a viable option. Some may even ask why, having made it back to my original family home, I wasn't tempted to stay. Surely the prospect of being back living with my father, no matter how removed that life was to me now, was preferable to returning back to Ireland, to living in care and to a situation with apparently even greater challenges?

The simple answer is, yes, part of me pined for parts of that life that seemed lost to me now. Walking into my old bedroom, a wave of memories and nostalgia washed over me, and for the briefest moment, I wanted to return to that time. But I couldn't go back. I couldn't turn back the hands of time and simply return to what was before. Too much had happened, too many twists, turns and experiences had occurred, and despite the pang of longing I felt for my previous life, I think I knew that it was exactly that – my *previous* life. I was a mother now, and although it was lovely to see so many friends and family, my life now was with Liam back in Ireland. My roots had grown there, and for all the pain and suffering I had gone through, Ireland was where I had become my own person, and it was where I had decided to forge the rest of my life.

I did wonder if I could make a life for us there, but as the trip drew to a close, I felt something that I hadn't felt in some time: homesickness. But it wasn't Nigeria or England I was homesick for this time; I had come to accept that, although these places were special, they were no longer home. Ireland was home now – home with Liam and our future, which stretched out in front of us. It was a future that wouldn't be possible without the sacrifices my mum had made for me and my siblings.

*

I had been attending a mixed school in Drumcondra since I moved into Sherrard House. When I found out I was pregnant, I told a close friend, and then everyone at school found out. I tried to deny it, but I had to keep running out of my English Junior Certificate paper with morning sickness, which pretty much confirmed it. So I stopped going to school after that because I just couldn't cope with the whispers and stares. When I was pregnant, Ciara paid for me to attend the Institute of Education for grinds so that I could sit my Junior Cert exams after I had Liam. I went on to complete my Junior Cert and Leaving Cert in a school called Margaret Aylward Community College in Whitehall in Dublin.

Margaret Aylward was a school that people went to if they didn't get into a school in Ballymun, Finglas or the general surrounding areas. It was a designated disadvantaged school, and it was the only school that would take me mid-year when I was doing my Junior Cert. It had a horrible brown uniform that was definitely not intended to be flattering, as is the norm with Catholic school uniforms. Having Liam had flicked a switch inside me, and I was determined to do well in school and get what I needed to go to college and pursue a career as an accountant. I had always enjoyed maths in school, and I had decided when I was really young that I wanted to become an accountant when I grew up.

One day, shortly after I started Fifth Year, my year head, who also happened to be my maths teacher, asked me to step outside her classroom so that she could speak to me privately. I was a bit wary – was I in trouble? Maths class was not something that I ever got called out of. For just a moment, I entertained the notion that I was about to receive praise, but I was quickly yanked back to reality. The teacher had not called me out to compliment me or to scold me. What occurred next took me completely by surprise. The teacher wanted to talk to me about my plans, or rather to outline a plan for me. She suggested that perhaps I should not skip Transition Year, but instead engage in it and enjoy one more year of school without the pressure of looming exams. She said that it would probably be a good idea, because, due to my recent acquisition of a child, it would be unlikely that I would be able to complete the Leaving Cert.

She was just trying to give me some advice informed by her experience with other girls in similar positions whom she had taught. While I was determined to do all I could to try to achieve my goal of becoming an accountant, I constantly had a voice in my head that asked, 'Who do you think you are to think you can do this?' Statistically, it was very, very, very unlikely that a single mother who got pregnant as a teenager and was being raised in residential state care was going to become an accountant. Who did I think I was to believe I could beat the odds? I wasn't a genius, and I wouldn't even have anywhere to live once I turned 18. Even with that narrative, I was determined to keep going and put my all into pursuing this goal until someone or something made it physically impossible. That determination came from the positive affirmations I received from Ciara, Paddy, Alan and Sherie.

But what about the single parent or young person in care who has the determination and ability to get through a degree but has teachers, family and friends telling them they are unlikely to be able to get through it based on their circumstances and all that they have been through? Who provides them with the positive affirmations to motivate them to overlook bias, believe in themselves and keep going? The answer is role models in their community who have persevered and are reaping the benefits. I needed to be that role model.

Although I had long since decided that accounting was what I wanted to do, I did change my mind a couple of times in Fifth and Sixth Year. At one point, I decided I wanted to be a primary school teacher so I could get three months off to spend time with Liam in the summer. But I had got an exemption from Irish when I moved to Ireland, which meant I couldn't pursue a primary school teaching course. With all the fights that happened in my school, the idea of becoming a secondary school teacher was nauseating, so that was out. Ultimately, though, I wanted myself and Liam to be financially secure, as I didn't have a family to fall back on, so I decided to pursue a reliable accounting qualification.

This was tough when I was the only kid staying back for after-school study, attending weekend grinds and creating study plans. With a baby at home, I wasn't going to have a thriving social life anyway, but it was tough to keep motivating myself when nobody else around me seemed to be doing the same. But then I met Ruth. She wanted to go to DCU to study journalism, and we bonded over study plans and shared class notes.

Due to its disadvantaged status, our school couldn't offer the wide range of subjects that students usually get to choose from when sitting their Leaving Cert. Ruth and I learned about a scholarship programme in DCU for students attending disadvantaged schools like ours. We worked out the minimum number of points we would need to receive to get into our respective desired courses under the scholarship programme and filled in our applications together. I attended grinds schools at the weekends for study notes, which I photocopied and shared with her. We were in this together, and we supported each other to get through the highs and lows of preparing for and sitting the Leaving Cert.

When the exams finally came around, Ruth was calm as a cucumber. I, on the other hand, started having panic attacks for the first time in my life. On the morning of the first English paper, I think I cried for two hours before I was able to start getting ready. I was inconsolable and convinced

I knew nothing about anything. But Debby came into my room and helped me to rationalise my fears about the exams determining the trajectory of the rest of my life. I calmed down after we discussed the worst-case scenario: I could repeat the exams the year after, or do a post-Leaving Cert course to help me to get into my desired accounting course in DCU.

I got through the exams in one piece and let my hair down the minute they were over. I loved spending the summer with Liam without worrying about exams in the back of my mind. But when results day came around, the panic started to creep in again.

It might not have seemed as big a day in Margaret Aylward as it was in more academically focused schools, but for me there was a lot riding on what was written in that little government-stamped envelope. Alan came with me to collect my results, but to my surprise, there were no other parents or guardians at the school. He waited at reception while my friends and I picked up our results. Ruth and I both got the points we had hoped for, and we were now looking forward to finding out if it was enough to get us our first-choice college places in DCU. I ran over to Alan to let him know and, to my complete surprise, he started crying. While I was disappointed that I wouldn't get to share that moment with my mum or dad, it meant the world to me that Alan was there, and that I could share it with him.

When our college offers came out, I thought I was dreaming when I saw that I got into DCU to study Accounting and Finance, my first choice. I called Ruth straight away to see if she had got good news too. I couldn't get through, so I presumed she was still sleeping. Later that afternoon, I got a text from her asking if I could talk. I called her and she seemed a bit quiet on the phone. She explained that she hadn't known how to tell me, but she hadn't qualified for the scholarship that would have helped us both get into DCU. She told me that she had forgotten to submit one part of the form, which meant that she was ineligible. She told me she would be going with her back-up plan, Coláiste Dhúlaigh, and that meant we wouldn't be attending DCU together as we had planned. I was honestly a little devastated and terrified to be going into that new world without her, but I couldn't imagine what she was going through. So I quickly steered the conversation towards more pressing matters – what to wear when we went out that night.

A letter to Debbie on turning 17

Debbie,

Being 17 was such an interesting year. You're still technically a child but getting ready to transition into adulthood. That transition doesn't usually come with an eviction notice, which makes this an even scarier time in your life. There's going to be so much change in the next year. Your support network won't be the same. You don't know how you'll cope without on-site babysitting. You don't know how you'll do studying accounting for the first time. But you've already come so far in just a few years. Just getting you to go to school used to be a challenge, and now you're getting ready to start college in a few months.

You don't need to go on this new journey alone. That's not what being an adult means. Ask for help when you need to, and try your best.

Lots of love,
Your future self x

Chapter 10

COLLEGE

'True resistance begins with people
confronting pain ... and wanting
to do something to change it.'

BELL HOOKS

While the idea of going to college was exciting, it was also terrifying. My 18th birthday was coming up, and that meant that the eviction date from my care home was also fast approaching. In 2010, when you turned 18 while in care, you were viewed as a fully functioning adult who should go on to thrive, with only the minimal support that Tusla wasn't even obligated to provide. I'd seen a lot of people turn 18 and have their supports ripped away from them before they were ready. Sometimes they fell in with the wrong group of friends, who replaced the artificial sense of something resembling a family that you can get when growing up in care. Some were even moved directly into homeless hostels after turning 18. Young people leaving care are, to this day, one of the groups most at risk of ending up homeless. I didn't want to have to go back into homeless hostels, especially now that I had Liam. After many sleepless nights worrying about this, I decided I was going to do everything in my power to take control of the situation so that my son and I wouldn't end up homeless.

I did a lot of research on what supports would be available to me and put together a budget. I also put together a plan for applying for supports. First, I went to the community welfare office to discuss the Back to Education Allowance, which I hoped would help me to pay for rent and essentials like food. Unfortunately, I was ineligible, because I wasn't going back to education – I had stayed in school. I was told that I would need to be out of education for a few years to be eligible. This was bizarre to me. In a few years I could have graduated and become a taxpayer! My best option was to stay on social welfare but not continue my education if I wanted to be able to receive a rent allowance. So I needed a miracle.

I met with my social worker, and she was adamant that they couldn't fund my rent and childcare supports while I was in college. She reiterated that I would need to stay out of education for a few years if that was my only option. My mum had loved writing strongly worded letters to people, asking to speak to managers, that type of thing. I used to find it so embarrassing, and couldn't understand why she didn't just let things go. But here I was facing a situation that I felt was worth fighting for.

I asked Ciara, Alan, Sherie, my teen-parent support worker and my aftercare worker (a support worker for kids coming out of care) to write letters in support of Tusla helping to fund my accommodation and childcare costs while I attended college. After I had gathered all the letters, I went online and looked for the email addresses of the CEO and CFO of Tusla. I sent them the letters with one of my own, explaining how I had worked hard to stay in school with a new baby. I pleaded with them for their support while I pursued my dream of becoming an accountant so that I could support myself and my child after transitioning out of care.

Within a couple of weeks of sending the email, my social worker requested a meeting with me and confirmed an aftercare package had been approved for me. The package would cover 90 per cent of my rent and 100 per cent of my childcare costs. I couldn't believe it! I was actually going to get to go to college! I am so thankful to every single person who helped me to secure the support I needed. When I say I couldn't have done this without them, I really mean it.

There is a 'grace period' between turning 18 and leaving care. There were just five weeks between my birthday and moving into my new home in north Dublin. I was leaving Dún na nÓg, leaving care, leaving Alan, Ciara, Paddy and all their team, and leaving what had grown to be an immense support network that had helped guide me through many great challenges. But I was also beginning my life as a student in college, beginning my life as a single mom out in the world and beginning my life as an adult. Although every single one of these things could be celebrated in their own way, they were no less terrifying for all of that.

Nicola, one of the social care workers from Dún na nÓg, dropped me off at the new house. She had already made numerous trips in her car bringing all my stuff over, but eventually she arrived for her final trip that day. The last bag of clothes, a card from all the staff, a hug and a wave from the car and there I was, alone in my new house. Well, not quite alone, as Liam was there too, of course, but for the first time ever, I was officially an adult and on my own.

On the one hand, there are aspects of living in care that will 'grow you up' in a hurry. I had experienced things that in many ways brought more naïve aspects of my childhood to an abrupt end, and, in some respects, made me extremely mature and capable. On the other hand, the care system can also institutionalise you and make you feel quite dependent on it. Living in care, you are never truly alone. You may be lonely, but you're never going to have the house to yourself. There are always staff around, day or night, and regardless of whether or not you are in a good place with them at any given moment, their constant presence is reassuring.

You can experience the deepest feeling of loneliness even in the middle of the biggest crowd, and although I now had my gorgeous son, who was fast approaching his third birthday, the feeling of being alone was very real to me. It might sound like an odd thing to say, but one of the things I ultimately loved about being pregnant was that sense of never being alone, of always having someone with me. I know I'm not alone in this, but my favourite thing to do while pregnant was to just sit quietly holding my bump. Liam had been a real kicker, and there were times when my bump resembled that scene in *Alien* where the creature bursts through his stomach, but I loved every part of that. Funnily enough, because he was such an active baby in the womb, I was extremely self-conscious when I was around people, thinking that everyone could see it, and I'm not one to draw attention to myself.

Those private moments when I could just relax and feel his presence inside me were truly magnificent. It's something that I truly miss. I can honestly say that whatever fears and anxiety I had around giving birth, I never felt lonely when I was pregnant. Although I was looking forward to starting my new life as a student, my main priority was still very much being the best mother I could be, and finding the right crèche for Liam was at the top of my list. After much searching, I eventually did find a place in a perfect crèche for Liam. Everything seemed to be falling into place.

I had gained entry to DCU through their access scholarship programme, and as such, they had organised a kind of orientation week for all the new access students to attend before the new term started. I hadn't given it much thought, other than that I'd had to turn down the offer of staying on campus for that week. I had Liam and was still living in care at the time, so I couldn't just move out for the week; I thought it would be better if I attended on a daily basis. I was also quite circumspect about telling people that I had a young child. I don't want that to sound like I was ashamed in any way of having my son, but I was cautious about who I shared that information with. Even with the best will in the world, people have a tendency to judge, and I was eager to present myself as a qualified candidate for a college education. I didn't want to be treated differently or as special from the get-go.

As it turned out, that orientation week was an absolute godsend in terms of setting my mind and my imposter syndrome at ease. I had failed to consider that any of the other access students might have similar stories to mine, or that they might have come from disadvantaged or dysfunctional backgrounds too. I'm not trying to say that everyone was in the same boat, but the other students on the access programme were lovely, and it came as such a relief that everyone was feeling similar things to me. I quickly realised that there was a good chance that, at least a couple of times a month, I could totally get away with wearing Penneys trackies.

That week gave me so much confidence and an understanding that the college experience wasn't about projecting a front, but rather about finding your own groove. I even shaved one side of my head at one point, thinking that would be all avant-garde and daring. Hey, we all learn from our mistakes!

The real revelation was that I would finally have a chance to define myself. For the last three years or so, I had been defined by my quest to get to where I was. In school, studying for my Leaving Cert, I had wanted to be seen as the good mother who also went to school. Here in college, I wanted to broaden those horizons, and develop not only a more nuanced sense of how I was perceived by my peers but also my own sense of self, who I was and who I was becoming. I definitely used this time to experiment and to explore who I really was, dodgy haircuts and all. I no longer had the support of the care system, but that also created a sense of freedom and individuality that simply cannot flourish in such stifling, and at times stigmatised, surroundings. Following that orientation week, I threw myself into college life when I could, and I would even go on to become a founder member of both the African and the Urban Arts societies in DCU.

Of course, my desire for personal growth and self-expression had to be tempered with a dose of realism. My morning routine consisted of getting both myself and Liam up, fed, washed and dressed before I left the house at 7.30 a.m. to walk him to his crèche. Once I had him settled there, I would get two buses to DCU. I didn't mind the journey, to be honest, it gave me some 'me' time to do my hair and make-up before getting to campus. After lectures, I'd leave in a hurry to get my buses home to ensure I could pick Liam up before the crèche closing time. Once we got home, he would hang out with me while I cooked dinner for us both. After dinner, he would play with toys in the sitting room while I camped out in the kitchen studying until bath time. After I put Liam to sleep, I would usually go downstairs and do more studying, depending on how close exams or assignment due dates were. I'd try to treat myself to at least half an hour of TV in my room after studying, which I usually fell asleep watching.

This routine is a good snapshot of what my life was like for the next few years. Liam was now three years old and full of beans. Sure, in the moments when you see your friends all making plans and talking about great nights out, you can't help but feel the pang of missing out, but I was always glad for the extra time to study. In fact, for the most part, I wasn't remotely jealous of anyone's social life. What really fired up my green-eyed monster was when people seemed to have endless time to go to the library and study.

If anything, the most challenging part of being a full-time student was avoiding becoming a part-time mom. In the three months after I gave birth, the scrutiny of my parenting skills in the form of the daily assessment carried out by staff really put me under pressure and, although I wouldn't admit it at the time, I was stressed that I would be judged to be a bad parent, a failure, unable to properly care for my own child. I don't need to explain that, from my own experience of parenting, this was a deeply ingrained and visceral fear. Could I lose my child to the care system just like my own mother before me? Now in college and living on my own, I was no longer afraid of judgement – but the spectre of failure still loomed large.

I wanted to be there for Liam, but I also had to balance that with why I was going to college in the first place: to build a better life for us. My education would give me the opportunity to do that and, in my darkest, most exhausted days, I would try to remind myself of that. It's what kept me going every time I got on the bus soaking wet, every time I missed a party, every dark morning and even darker night. Every time I had a little cry, I would remind myself why I was doing all of it and that gave me the strength to keep going.

Sherie was always there for me – and I mean always. Whether it was her regular check-ins or me crying down the phone at 3 a.m. the day before an exam, she never turned me away or told me that she was too busy. The remarkable thing about this is that I know she had many people like me in her life who needed her in the same way. She was truly the most selfless and generous person that I've had the pleasure of knowing, and without her, I simply wouldn't have made it through college.

Three years after leaving care and moving out on my own, six years after becoming a mother and five years since the loss of my own, I graduated from DCU with a 2.1 degree in Accounting and Finance. On that day, I had job offers from two of the four biggest accounting firms in the world, and I received a scholarship from the largest company in Ireland to complete a master's degree in accounting. But the most special part for me was being able to share the day with Ciara, Alan, Sherie, my dad, my big brother, my baby brother and my son – the people who had believed in me when I sometimes didn't believe in myself.

A letter to Debbie on graduation day

Debbie,

When you started college you had so many worries about whether you'd be able to complete your course. You had never done accounting before going to college, but today you are graduating with an honours degree in Accounting and Finance. You did this on your own with a toddler. Your biggest worry when you were studying for exams was about how much time you were spending with your head stuck in a book and the impact that would have on Liam. But he couldn't be prouder of you today. He's a great kid who has benefited hugely from growing up watching you study. You rarely enjoy a moment like this, and you're already thinking about what's next. My advice to you is to take a minute to celebrate all the hard work you've put in paying off.

Lots of love,
Your future self x

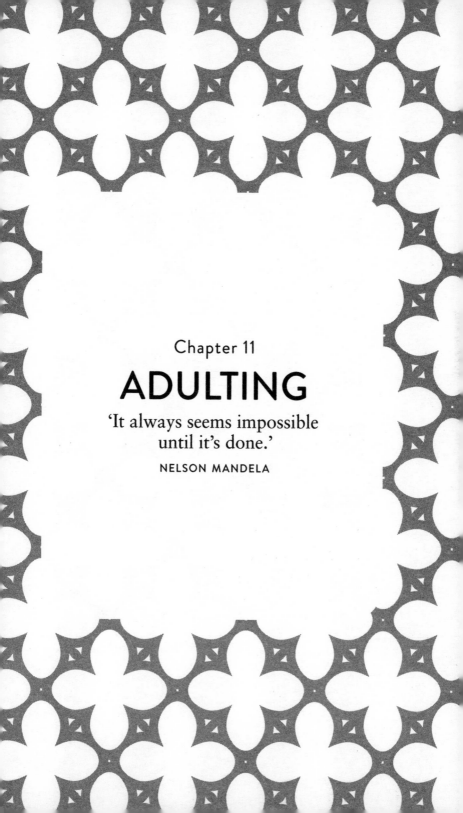

Chapter 11

ADULTING

'It always seems impossible
until it's done.'

NELSON MANDELA

Although I had my degree, my journey to becoming a qualified chartered accountant was only beginning. A few years previously, when I had attended the open day on the DCU campus – and instantly fell in love with it – I had spoken to the head of the accounting course who advised me about the different types of accounting qualifications and the different routes to obtaining them. In order to qualify as a chartered accountant, I needed to complete CAP1, CAP2 and FAE exams. I also needed to simultaneously complete a three-and-a-half-year training contract with an accounting firm.

The Accounting and Finance degree allowed me to receive exemptions from CAP1 exams. Completing a master's in accounting would provide CAP2 exam exemptions, shorten the training period to three years and attract a slightly higher salary. I knew that a training position in an accounting firm would require me to put in a lot of late nights, which I would need to balance with raising a young son and studying for my professional exams. So the master's route was the most preferable for me, as I would only need to do that juggling routine for one year while I completed my FAEs, compared to two years of juggling study while I completed my CAP2 and FAE exams. But how was I going to pay for a master's? I put this question to the back of my mind until I was nearing the end of my degree.

The big four accounting firms (EY, Deloitte, KPMG and PwC) recruit hundreds of graduates each year, primarily into their audit departments, during a process called the 'milk round'. There were a handful of positions available for consulting graduates, and these roles were like gold dust because they didn't come with the same promise of working 80-hour weeks during busy periods, as auditing roles did. At the beginning of the final year of my degree, I researched scholarship programmes and grants that would help to fund a master's in accounting in DCU, but there were none available. I decided to try to apply for one of the coveted consulting graduate spots but, unfortunately, I didn't even get an interview for any of the roles I applied for.

I was disheartened, and it was tough going through my final year without a graduate job or a guarantee of a place in the master's programme. Cathy McLoughlin from the access office on campus helped to lift my spirits by reassuring me that I had got this far against all odds. She asked me to focus on getting through my final year and worry about 'what next?' after I finished my exams. This was the best advice I could have received, and it helped me to stay focused on the academic marathon I had to run. This was one of many times that Cathy and the support offered by the access programme helped me to stay focused on completing my degree when I got demotivated.

After I got my final-year exam results, I knew I would be graduating with an honours degree, so without any further hesitation, I applied for a master's and was duly accepted. There was just one minor problem: I had absolutely no idea how I was going to pay for it. There have been times in my life when I've just kept moving forward in the hope that solutions would present themselves and, for the most part, that has turned out to be the case. A lot of the time the solutions came from the generosity of others, and occasionally from a happy accident.

I figured that I could get a loan from the credit union and at the same time investigate what, if any, new financial supports were potentially available. As it turned out, there was a new scholarship, sponsored by Cement Roadstone Holdings, being offered to master's students in DCU. At the time I thought it was a long shot, particularly with my recent record of unsuccessful job applications, but to my absolute joy and relief, I was accepted. Between the loan and my scholarship, I was able to pursue my master's. I couldn't believe it!

During the next set of milk rounds in October 2014, I applied for graduate roles in auditing, as there were more roles available in that area. Yes, auditing wasn't my first choice, but I knew it was possible to transfer to consulting after I completed my training contract if I worked hard and made the right impressions with the right people. To my sheer delight, I received job offers from two of the big four accounting firms.

The following year, I graduated from DCU with a high 2.1 master's degree in Accounting. I had started in my new role two weeks before, and I was loving it. All incoming graduates had been invited to the office a few months before to meet with people working in various departments. We were then asked to rank in order which department we most wanted to work for. I ranked banking and aircraft leasing first, and to my delight, I received an offer to join this team. I was so eager to impress and prove myself as a high performer from the first day. If anyone needed me to work late or at the weekend, I happily obliged. Thankfully, my manager was aware I was a single mum, so I was allowed to bring my work home with me so that I could be there for crèche pick-up time. My busiest months were between December and February, so I tried to plan ahead, and of course I leaned on the network of friends who helped me look after Liam if I had to work late.

Sherie was always there for me when I needed her, and she was there for so many people who used the family counselling service where she worked. We frequently worried about how much the other was working or studying. When she got run down with a really bad cough, she initially thought it was just her body asking her to slow down. We spoke on the phone frequently, and I started getting worried when she didn't seem to be getting any better. At some stage, she went to the doctor, who told her she had pneumonia.

I was so worried when I heard. Sherie was basically a second mother to me, and I just wanted to be able to do anything I could to help her feel better. Then one day, while we sat having coffee in one of her favourite spots in George's Street Arcade, she told me she had been diagnosed with cancer. I didn't know anyone who had had cancer before, and I was terrified of losing her. She told me that they had caught it at a very early stage and that the doctors didn't even think she would need chemo, so I wasn't to worry. Over the next few months that changed, and eventually she had difficulty breathing, needed chemo and lost her hair.

And then, one day in the middle of February 2017, I was waiting for a bus home from work when I received a call from Sherie's colleague in the counselling service. My beautiful friend, counsellor and mentor had died. I think she tried to protect me by not telling me how sick she actually was towards the end of her life. That's just the type of person she was, always thinking about others. She was the most caring and kind human being I have ever met, and I feel so lucky to have had her in my life. I hadn't cried at my mom's funeral because I think I was still in shock, but I bawled my eyes out at Sherie's funeral.

Sherie had been like a mother to me when my own had passed and even before that, when I needed a friendly shoulder to cry on as a confused, pregnant 14-year-old. Always available, always at the end of the phone, she got me through some awful moments at times by just being there. But Sherie was not just a reassuring presence. She was a towering mountain of inspirational womanhood.

We bonded over many things. She had been a young single mum and had lost a parent as a teenager. She never judged me and only ever tried to guide me based on her own experiences, which made me trust her instantly. Her obituary in the *Irish Times* said: 'A bit of a maverick, she would always do what she felt was right for the client even if it meant bending conventional rules of therapy. She had an incredible aura of empathy that enabled her to give hugely without diminishing herself. Clients talked of being simultaneously enveloped and set free by her. Always smiling and exuding a sense of reassurance, she revelled in humour both to deliver wisdom with a laugh and to also deploy a caustic observation.'

I have never seen so many people gathered together for a funeral. The crowds that turned out that day were living proof of the heartfelt and significant impact that this gorgeous soul had had on people's lives. It's unfortunate that the true measure of a person's life is often displayed in their absence, but in Sherie's case it was entirely appropriate, as she would have run a mile from such an event in her honour.

After her funeral, I took the time to read a book she'd sent me in May 2015 called *We Should All Be Feminists* by Chimamanda Ngozi Adichie. On the first page Sherie had written, 'A book for one extraordinary African Irish UK woman by another great African American UK woman!' As I read the book, it was like every sentence was speaking directly to me. This is when I decided I wanted to try to help people in the same way Sherie had helped me and so many others. I just needed to figure out how best to do that.

A letter to Debbie after Sherie's passing

Debbie,

I know you're hurting after the loss of Sherie. She has been in your life since you were 14. I know you're worried that you won't be able to deal with any challenges you face in the future without her advice. But over the years Sherie has given you the tools you needed to manage challenges on your own. You'll be okay. You now have two angels watching over you in heaven, Sherie and your mum.

Lots of love,
Your future self x

Chapter 12

SHARING
MY STORY

'Freeing yourself was one thing,
claiming ownership of that freed
self was another.'

TONI MORRISON, *BELOVED*

M ost people don't tune into the show *First Dates* for the dynamic insights it offers into social activism. Strangely, however, in a very round-about way it helped to lead me into the arena of social activism and philanthropic entrepreneurship.

The show is a reality TV programme that sets strangers up on blind dates, which is filmed, edited and then broadcast as light entertainment. The show first aired in the UK back in 2013, and I instantly became hooked. I started watching it when I was in college, as it was the perfect 'chewing gum for your brain' type of programme for unwinding with at the end of the day. Like most reality TV shows, the appeal lies in either empathising with or distancing yourself from the protagonists, from love at first sight to the inevitable car crash moments when it all goes horribly wrong. Either way, it all combines to be fairly addictive viewing.

I'm not going to lie – at heart, I'm a die-hard old romantic, and my favourite moments on the show were when people really connected and found a genuine spark of attraction and, dare I say, the beginnings of true love. For me, there really is nothing nicer than seeing two people find each other like that and begin to build a life together. Also, despite the odds against it, I liked the idea that someone else could do all the legwork for you and all you had to do was just show up in a nice frock to meet your true love. Who wouldn't like that fantasy?

Needless to say, when they announced an Irish version of the show, I was super excited to throw my hat into the ring. At least that was my initial reaction: 'Oh my God, *First Dates Ireland*, I have to go for it!' I filled out the online application and sent it in, but I didn't really think about it too much, not least because I figured that it was the longest of long shots that I would get chosen anyway. It wasn't until they got back to me requesting a self-taped audition that I began to consider the possibility that I could actually be picked to go on the programme. I also started to question whether or not this was even something that I should be seriously considering. The fantasy of going on a dating show, meeting Prince Charming and living happily ever after is one thing when you're sitting at home eating a bowl of popcorn in your pyjamas, but quite another when the possibility of your private life being put on display on national television starts to become more real.

Ironically, I was actually on a date with someone I had been casually seeing when I got the email from the producers saying that they wanted me to tape something. Without really considering it, I asked my date if he thought it was a good idea – at the very least I thought it would be good manners to ask his opinion. Let's just say that his non-committal response was a motivating factor in going ahead with the tape. I certainly wasn't finding true love at that table. I sent in the tape, and before I knew it, they had got back to me and informed me that I had passed that round and that they now wanted me to come in for a more formal audition. This is when the alarm bells really started ringing. It was all getting very real, and given that my life had only just started to settle down after such an eventful and at times painful journey, did I really want to risk putting all that into the public spotlight? I had to ask myself this question not only from a personal perspective and the effect it might have on Liam, but equally I had to consider the impact that such exposure might have on my professional life. Some of my closest friends were aware of my life history and circumstances, but it was certainly not something I had discussed openly in my work environment.

I was chosen, and I overcame my initial fears about going on the programme, swept along as I was by the excitement of the whole adventure. Little did I know that the anxiety I had experienced before the show was nothing compared to what I would feel after it was recorded.

The show is recorded on location in the Gibson Hotel at the Point Village, only a couple of Luas stops away from where I was working at the time. In terms of what the audience sees, the action is fairly straightforward. We see people arriving for their date, their little chat with the friendly barman and then the date itself, followed by a short interview, which includes the all-important 'Well, would you like to see each other again?' question, and then finally the departure, which in some cases has seen couples bailing into a taxi together with giggles of 'the night is young' and a gleam in their eyes.

The reality of shooting all this, though, is a lot more clunky and time-consuming. My 'arrival' was actually filmed long after I had originally arrived, as they have to check you in and set up the shot, etc. The other thing that they do is try to grease the wheels a little with some alcohol. I'm not saying that they're plying you with drinks from the minute you arrive, but they certainly are available and encouraged. I was prepared for this – I knew from watching the show that I would need to be very careful in this regard. Now that I'm a bit older and wiser I don't drink that much. I didn't want to let my guard down and say the wrong thing, which might have happened if I had had too much to drink.

I would say that this was definitely in the top two worst dates I've ever been on. You know Aidan in *Sex and the City* – the sexy but reliable guy? That was who I asked for. Instead, I ended up on a date with a much sleazier version of Mr Big. In his pre-date interview, he bragged that he had never been rejected by a woman! Insert eye-roll here. One of the first questions he asked me was where I went to school, and the man was in his late 20s! Of course, anyone from Dublin knows that the only people who still ask these types of questions are people who went to private school and can't wait to tell you so. I'm not a part of that world, so the name of the school didn't impress me much.

He told me that he and his friends had only applied to the show for a laugh, but that he was the only one who had made it through – super romantic. He also apparently had a list of attributes for some imaginary dream girlfriend. As the date progressed he would say 'that's a tick' every once in a while, like he was comparing my attributes against this list. It was really quite annoying. We definitely weren't a match and didn't see each other again after that.

From a romance point of view, my *First Dates* experience had not been a success. But thankfully, the response I received, both directly from friends and on social media, was overwhelmingly positive. I genuinely hadn't gone on the show so that I could use that platform to talk about my experience and how it related to other pertinent social issues. I'd just wanted to have an adventure and maybe meet a nice guy. The fact that people now wanted to talk to me about the other aspects of my life, like what it was like being homeless as a kid, was a daunting surprise.

Each year the big accounting firms create marketing campaigns that they use to recruit students during milk rounds. They would put up posters and leave brochures all over college campuses for students to try to visualise what working for them would be like. Every year, I stared at the women in those campaigns and just thought, 'Wow! I'm never going to be as put together and perfect as them.' I really looked up to the women who appeared in those campaigns. In my second year of training, my company asked me to appear in their graduate recruitment brochure. I couldn't believe it!

When the brochures came out, I don't know why, but it was one of the first times I took stock of how far I had come. Lefroy House, that first homeless hostel I stayed in, was on the same street as my new prestigious workplace. Less than 10 years before, I had been trying to get a bed in that hostel. But now, I had a degree and a master's in accounting, and I was working for one of the biggest accounting firms in the world. Out of more than 2,000 people who worked in the building, they had chosen me to appear in that brochure, and it meant the absolute world to me. In a reflective moment, I emailed every single person and organisation that had helped me along the way to say that Liam and I would be eternally grateful for all they had done.

Around the same time, my *First Dates* appearance aired. Hoping that my story would help to change how people perceived a person living in homelessness, Focus Ireland emailed me back to ask if I would feature in a fundraising campaign. While I had shared personal facts about myself when I appeared on *First Dates*, this wasn't going to be easy for me. I worked in a conservative environment, and I didn't know how people would react to the news that I used to be homeless. I was scared of potentially destroying my career before it had really begun. I asked if I could take some time to think about the request.

The homelessness crisis in Ireland had only got worse in recent years. My understanding of its root cause was that the Irish government had previously built houses for people requiring financial support, called social housing. In the recession, it tried to delegate this to the private sector. The private sector, however, wasn't interested in building social housing on the same scale, which created long social housing waiting lists. Meanwhile, due to a lack of supply of new homes to buy, demand for homes to rent kept increasing, and with it, rent prices kept rising. Eventually, the country got to a situation where single parents with young kids were facing €1,000 rent increases from their landlords, and they had no way of paying for this extra amount. This led to evictions, and families were forced to share a room in temporary housing until they could find somewhere else to live. This could take two years, or sometimes even longer.

Every time I heard a young child on the radio talking about their experience in homeless accommodation, I got a feeling of déjà vu and overwhelming sadness. I heard some of my more privileged friends talk about the homelessness crisis, but it usually wasn't with empathy. They would often place the blame on the homeless person and what they had done to end up in their situation. 'They would probably have money for rent if they didn't spend it on drugs. Where are the fathers? They should pay the rent.' What these points of view failed to consider is that the children in these situations had done nothing wrong. They were being robbed of their childhoods in these cramped spaces, and going to school carrying burdens they were too young to fully understand. I would get into these passionate debates, but my friends couldn't understand where it was coming from, because I hadn't shared much of my background with them.

I'd also been looking for a way to help people since losing Sherie, but I wasn't sure how. I decided that sharing my story once, with a small group of donors, would be a tiny way to try to help change how people perceived our homelessness crisis and its victims. I accepted Focus Ireland's request to share my story with a small group of female potential donors.

Writing the speech for that event was a really emotional experience. I had to reflect on my life from the start and how much I had had to deal with when I was just a child. I cried while writing every word. I practised the speech many times over in preparation for the event. But the thought of speaking at the event itself made me feel physically sick. I kept worrying in case it was a massive mistake. I didn't want people to feel sorry for me and see me as some poor homeless girl. I had worked so hard to try to build a new life for me and Liam, so why was I now looking back?

I asked Ciara and Alan to come along to the event for moral support, and they assured me I was doing something that could really make a difference. When it was my turn to speak, I felt the nerves return but tried to focus on just getting through the speech. As I got halfway through the speech, the tears started rolling down my face; I couldn't stop them. As I talked about each stage of my journey, the feelings of hopelessness that had swept over me at the time came back. The gratitude I felt for everyone who helped me overwhelmed me. I felt I was messing up the speech with my blubber, and I tried to just get through it as quick as I could.

When I finished, I looked up expecting to see a lot of bored and disappointed faces, but instead everyone got to their feet to give me a round of applause, and they all had tears in their eyes too. People kept coming up to me telling me how inspirational and resilient I was, which meant the world to me. But had I made an impact? Focus Ireland managed to raise over €12,000, and they told me it had been one of their most successful breakfast fundraising events. I couldn't believe how much of an impact talking about myself for a few minutes had made.

Following on from that talk and the positive feedback from it, Focus Ireland asked me to take part in other fundraising and public speaking events on their behalf. If this was how I could help in some way to support young people experiencing homelessness, I felt it would be selfish of me not to do it just because I was scared of what people would think of me. And so, if I could get time off from work, I accepted the invitations.

The Youth Summit was one of the events that I was fortunate enough to speak at. It was an event held in the RDS that brought together children from youth clubs around the country. Many in attendance were kids living in care too. I felt really lucky to get to share my story with them, and hoped they would get inspired to go to college if they weren't already considering this option. I stayed for a little bit after my talk to answer any questions the kids had on accessing the same supports I had, or on overcoming the challenges I had faced. As I was heading home, the organisers approached me and asked if I would mind doing a couple of interviews as part of the event. I nervously accepted, and rationalised that they would probably be tiny pieces in a newspaper or something that nobody I knew would read.

The first interview turned out to be a big feature piece in the *Irish Times*, so that was the end of trying to share my story with only a small group of people. The second was a very short slot on *Drivetime* on Newstalk that producers for both Ryan Tubridy's radio show and *The Late Late Show* heard. When I was invited on to both, I honestly couldn't understand what was happening. I kept pinching myself to make sure I wasn't dreaming.

I simply cannot say enough good things about my experience of meeting Ryan Tubridy. He was so kind, so patient and so reassuring. He and his producers understood how absolutely terrifying this experience was for me, and they helped to create safe environments to put me at ease while sharing my story with hundreds of thousands of people across the country. The response I received was overwhelming, and the more empathetic narrative that emerged around our homelessness crisis showed me how much of an impact I could have. But it wasn't enough. I knew that I needed to do more than just talk about myself.

*

At Sherie's funeral, I had been shocked by how full the church was – full of people whose lives Sherie had had a remarkable impact upon. She

had been there to comfort me when I was convinced that I would fail an exam, or that I was a
terrible parent because I was studying too much.
But it seemed like she provided this same timely
comfort to half of Dublin, and I don't know how
the woman found the time. And it had got me
thinking about what I would leave behind when I
was gone. Yes, I was only 24, but I knew I wanted
to work really hard, no matter the cost, to become
a partner or a C-suite executive at a large mul-
tinational company one day – that had been my
goal. But after the funeral it struck me that, if
this was the extent of my ambition, I wouldn't
get to make the type of impact on people's lives
that Sherie did. My goal was still to work hard
to become a partner or get the C-suite job, but it
was equally important to me to try to help people.
Specifically, I wanted to try to find a way to help
Black immigrants in Ireland, single parents and
young people coming out of state care like me.

As I became more visible at public speaking
events, I started to hear more and more first-hand
accounts about Black immigrants experiencing discrimination, which impacted their ability to secure

employment or progress in their organisations. I started to educate myself on the facts behind these accounts. For example, in 2009, the Equality Authority and the Economic and Social Research Institute found that candidates with Irish names were more than twice as likely to be invited to interview for advertised jobs as candidates with identifiably non-Irish names, even though both submitted equivalent CVs. In 2018, the Irish Human Rights and Equality Commission and the Economic and Social Research Institute found that Black non-Irish people were five times more likely to experience discrimination when seeking employment in Ireland when compared to White Irish people. They also found that Black non-Irish people are over two and a half times more likely to experience discrimination when in employment compared to White Irish people.

When I became aware of these issues, I couldn't just look away and say that it was somebody else's problem. I decided to play my part by mentoring Black immigrants, referring them for roles and advocating for them on the diversity committees I sat on. At the time of writing, I'm working with

Chartered Accountants Ireland to launch its first network for students and members from ethnic minority communities and their allies. The network will focus on impactful initiatives that create a more inclusive and diverse professional environment for all accountants, for example, by issuing guidance for companies on how to ensure that their policies don't unfairly discriminate against hiring people from ethnic minority backgrounds. It still doesn't feel like enough, but it's a start.

In relation to helping single parents and young people coming out of state care, my inspiration came from Catherine McAuley. In January 2018, I was waiting for a bus home from work and decided to look up the building across the road. It had a nun's statue outside, and I thought it was a strange location for a convent because it was so close to the city centre. The statue, it turned out, was of Catherine McAuley, who had been a poor orphan who went to work for a family friend on their estate in Coolock in the early 1800s.

When the family friend died, they had no other relatives, so Catherine inherited their estate. She could have taken that money and gone on to live the really nice life she had definitely earned. Instead, one of the first things she did with the money was to open the building that I saw in front of me. In this building, she helped to provide accommodation and education to other orphans. That became her life's work, supporting others who had grown up with similar disadvantages to her based on her own understanding of their needs. She sounded like an incredible woman. I started thinking about the type of impact I could make based on my own experiences.

Getting a place in college had been hard enough. Not being able to easily access accommodation and childcare while I completed my degree didn't make things any easier. It was a constant worry, while I completed my Leaving Cert, that I wouldn't be able to take up a college place even if I did get in. I was worried that I wouldn't have a place to live and/or wouldn't be able to afford childcare. I had to lobby a government agency, using references from people from multiple agencies, to get access to funding for accommodation and childcare while I was in college. While I was awarded this on an exceptional basis, I think of all the vulnerable people who needed that same level of support but didn't get it. Every time I think about it I feel terribly guilty that I got lucky. So when I started public speaking, people kept asking me, how can we support other vulnerable young people who come from disadvantaged backgrounds to complete their third-level education and secure higher-paying jobs? There wasn't one answer to that question. While you could donate money to educational support programmes, those programmes couldn't build houses and offer crèche places to their service users.

So I kept this idea at the back of my mind – one day, I would buy a big Georgian building and let single parents who were attending college live there rent-free. I would also include a crèche on the ground floor so they could access childcare for free. I would have *loved* something like this when I was going to college, partly because of the community support: one mum could support another based on shared experiences and hardships. After I shared my story on *The Late Late Show* in January 2018, I was overwhelmed with a significant amount of survivor's guilt. So I poured that into this idea, thinking – why not try to bring it to life now?

I wrote the idea on my phone and started a petition straight away. In a short period of time, we had gathered over 12,000 signatures and hundreds of comments from women saying this would make a big impact on their lives. I put together a business plan and invited a number of charities and government agencies to a presentation. Feedback from those who attended was mixed – some people committed their support to the idea, but others felt the idea that single parents would want to not only go to college but also succeed there was ridiculous. I was so frustrated with this very biased way of thinking. I was down and felt defeated for a few days, but after some pep talks from people like Ciara, I dusted myself off and made a plan for my next steps.

I approached the Community Foundation, who reached out to their donors with the idea. Most felt that that project was at too early a stage to support yet, but one woman offered to meet with me to discuss the idea. The prospective supporter was an incredible woman who had been recognised previously as a leading philanthropist. I met with her and chatted to her about the problem I was trying to solve – a lack of access to accommodation and childcare acting as a barrier to third-level education for single parents. I told her that the impact of this was that they were more vulnerable to living in consistent poverty with their children, because without degrees they could only access low-paying jobs.

In comparison, a single parent with a degree was much less likely to end up experiencing deprivation. This is before you even factor in the housing crisis, which is pushing more and more single-parent families into homeless accommodation. The solution was simple: put forward the supports that are required in one location. Provide accommodation and childcare (along with wraparound supports, like access to mentoring, counselling and grinds) to single parents with the determination and ability to successfully complete their degrees. The prospective donor was impressed, and straightaway pledged a donation of €500,000. This idea had finally become real! Someone believed in it! Someone believed in me!

I started a charity called Empower the Family to bring the idea to life. After we got everything set up, a friend of mine connected me with an incredible man called Ben, who led the Housing Department in Dublin City Council. I discussed our plans with him, and he thought it was a great idea that would make a big impact on people's lives. He recommended that we partner with an approved housing body to deliver the housing element of the plan. But none of the housing bodies were interested in partnering with me on the idea. So I decided to form a strong board of directors with the experience required to start my own approved housing body. I had got this far, why give up now?

And that's exactly what I did. The Finance Director for Google Ireland was one of our first directors. Alan, Ciara and her mum, Mary, also came on board, and the Development Director for Ronan Group Developments came on too. We secured letters of support from Dublin City Council and the Irish Council for Social Housing and gained Approved Housing Body status from the Department of Housing, Planning and Local Government. As I write this, we are working with Dublin City Council to acquire a site in Ballymun, where we will deliver Ireland's first Social Student Housing Development. The planned development will provide accommodation and childcare to single parents and young people who are coming out of state care and entering into third-level education.

I'm still very young, but I'm in a more fortunate position than a lot of people I grew up with. I wrote this book to share my experience of what it was like growing up in care. I hope people can understand how easy it is to slip through the cracks. If you were to take away just one thing, it should be that one good adult can have a transformational impact on a vulnerable child's life, simply by believing in them. .

A letter to my 65-year-old self

Debbie,

I hope Liam has grown up to be a kind man. I hope Empower the Family has been able to provide housing and childcare to people who need it throughout Ireland. And I hope you've lived a happy and fulfilled life.

Lots of love,
Your 28-year-old self x

RESOURCES

EPIC (www.epiconline.ie) aims to advance the interests and welfare of children and young adults in the care system by advocating on their behalf.

Jigsaw (www.jigsaw.ie) offers expert mental health advice and support, online and in person, to young people aged 12–25.

One Family (www.onefamily.ie) provides free, confidential, non-judgemental and HSE-approved information, support and counselling on all options during an unplanned pregnancy and after abortion.

Samaritans (www.samaritans.org) offers listening and support to people and communities in times of need.

ACKNOWLEDGEMENTS

Thank you so much to my agent, Faith O'Grady, and everyone at Gill, especially Nicki, Aoibheann, Teresa, Laura, Chloe, Claire, Charlie, Fiona and Kristen, for giving me the opportunity to write this book and all your support and guidance while writing it.